THE 101 BEST

Aquarium Plants

THE ADVENTUROUS AQUARIST™ GUIDE SERIES

Produced and distributed by:

T.F.H. Publications, Inc.
One T.F.H. Plaza
Third and Union Avenues
Neptune City, NJ 07753
www.tfh.com

Printed and bound in China
11 12 13 14 15   3 5 7 9 8 6 4

ISBN-13: 978-1-890087-19-7
ISBN-10: 1-890087-19-X
UPC-A: 6-81290-8719-5

Library of Congress Cataloging-in-Publication Data
Sweeney, Mary Ellen.
1952–
The 101 best aquarium plants : how to choose and keep hardy, vibrant, eye-catching species that will thrive in your home aquarium / by Mary E. Sweeney ; principal photography by George Farmer ... [et al.].
p. cm. -- (Adventurous aquarist guide) (Microcosm/TFH professional series)
Includes bibliographical references.
ISBN 1-890087-19-X
1. Aquarium plants. 2. Aquariums. 3. Aquarium plants--Pictorial works. 4. Aquariums--Pictorial works. I. Title.
SF457.7.S94 2008
639.34--dc22   2008007824

Designed by Linda Provost | Color by Digital Engine
A MICROCOSM/TFH Professional Series Book

Co-published by:

TFH Publications, Inc.
Neptune City, NJ 07753
www.tfh.com

Microcosm, Ltd.
Charlotte, VT 05445
www.microcosm-books.com

THE 101 BEST

Aquarium Plants

How to Choose Hardy, Vibrant, Eye-Catching Species That Will Thrive in Your Home Aquarium

Mary E. Sweeney

Photography

George Farmer, Neil Hepworth,
Aaron Norman, Jeff Ucciardo, Ben Tan,
Diana Walstad, Matthew L. Wittenrich

MICROCOSM

tfh

PROFESSIONAL
SERIES™

A Microcosm Edition

WWW.MICROCOSM-BOOKS.COM

To Eamonn

When you were very new, we used to sit in front of the tank and rock. You followed the movement of the fishes in the water before you could see me even.

When you were three, we went fishing with the Doctor and you caught the first fish. At four you knew exactly how much brine shrimp baby discus should have (and never let me give them more). You're always the first to see a change in our aquaria. You swim, you row. You sure took to the water, didn't you?

You're a throwback, son, a real keeper.

ACKNOWLEDGEMENTS

I would like to extend my immense gratitude to: Ben Tan, Matt Wittenrich, Neale Monks, Neil Hepworth, George Farmer, Robert Hudson, Brad McLane, Tim Pfeffer, Jeff Ucciardo, Aaron Norman, and Diana Walstad. Without you, and all your glorious images, there'd be no book.

Who could ever forget the aquarium society faithfuls who inspire and encourage all would-be writers, editors, speakers, and fish show judges, and who have been the inspirations for this and any book I ever write. I include some special friends made through aquarium societies, Mary Bailey, Ginny Eckstein, and Karen Randall. For always, always encouraging me, thanks to my genuine friend and mentor, Dr. Herbert R. Axelrod and my colleagues, Neal Pronek, Dr. Warren Burgess, Lourdes Burgess, Jerry Walls, Ray Hunziker, John Quinn, and Dr. Stan Weitzmann. All the authors whose manuscripts have filled my working life have also left their impressions and helped to form who I am now, and I thank you.

I am extremely appreciative of the work of the Microcosm team, especially Linda Provost, Emily Stetson, Judith Billard, Matthew Wittenrich, and James Lawrence. Thanks also to the folks at T.F.H. Publications, especially Craig Sernotti, for helping this effort come to fruition.

Thanks also to my big family for not thinking it too odd that I should carry aquaria from state to state when I moved about "finding myself." Anyone who knows me knows how strong the connection is between my vocation in aquaria and life on the Jersey Shore. Our family's ties to the coastal waters on both sides of the Atlantic and intimate involvement with fish as a way of life was introduced to me early, and I shall never forget the first time I peered over the side of a curragh to see a whole metropolis below in the clear waters off the Irish coast. Growing up on stories of salmon runs, selkies, and, of course, the sale of "Cockles and Mussels," it is very clear to me how we are all connected to the water and all the life within it. Finally, thanks for John Sweeney, my spouse, who is so much to me in all things, but in this for his eagle eye that keeps the typos at bay and a bit of egg off my face.

Mary E. Sweeney
Highlands, New Jersey

CONTENTS

Aquascape Styles, page 178

Meant as a field guide to freshwater aquarium plant species, this handbook uses color photographs taken in home aquaria and in the wild for quick visual identification. Species appearing here have been selected as outstanding for their hardiness and durability in aquarium conditions, for their attractiveness, and for their availability to freshwater enthusiasts.

Plants are arranged alphabetically by genus and species with common names on the line beneath.

Subheadings within species accounts contain concise reference material, advice, and comments, and where applicable are arranged as follows:

SCIENTIFIC NAME

This is the most current name applied to the plant by the scientific community. The name is in the form of a binomial. The first name indicates the genus to which the plant belongs, while the second is the species name; for example, *Microsorum pteropus* (Java Fern).

COMMON NAME

At least one common name is listed for each species. Common names with the widest acceptance in the aquarium plant hobby are used. The first name provided is the name most frequently used in the authoritative checklists and field guides written by botanists. In assigning the preferred common name to each species, we have attempted to steer away from obvious misnomers and toward names that will minimize confusion and bring science and hobby closer together.

OVERVIEW

Here is the a brief introduction to each plant, with its most important attributes and with information about its discovery, development, and availability.

HABITAT

This entry describes the environmental conditions where the plant occurs naturally. Information about the native biotope provides clues to how to best keep and reproduce botanical specimens.

The flowers of Aponogeton offer clues to the identity of the different species in this genus. The size and shape of the leaves are often very similar, but the flowers tell the tale. Here they nod above the floating duckweed that adorns this quiet pond.

NATIVE RANGE

Distribution or native range notes the broad geographical area where each species occurs. The distribution of a plant is of great value to those aquarists wishing to set up a tank that represents a natural community from a certain geographical region. Clues about keeping the plant successfully often can be found in descriptions of the conditions where the plant is known to thrive in nature.

MAXIMUM HEIGHT

This is the vertical distance from the substrate to the tips of the leaves of each plant species. Because all plants do not grow in the same direction, a 1-inch-high plant could spread quite a distance from its point of origin. Keep in mind that it is not only the height that gives the plant its size: the spread of the leaves can create a considerable footprint in some species.

LIGHTING

Lighting is a critically important element to plants. The intensity of the light and the photoperiod are major determinants of success or failure with aquatic plants. Low-light plants can tolerate as low as 1 watt of light per gallon; moderate-light plants need 2 to 3 watts per gallon, and bright-light plants need 4 to 5 watts per gallon.

WATER

Water temperature, pH, and water hardness are crucial to aquarium plants' viability. The range of temperatures given represents seasonal and night/day variations in nature as well as temperature observations of collectors, nurseries, hobbyists, and botanists.

FEEDING

Though aquarium plants use light and carbon dioxide as food, they need different levels of macro- and micronutrients as well. Some plants are heavy root feeders and benefit from a fertilized substrate. Other plants gather their sustenance through the leaves or even from the water through nodal roots that grow from the internodes on the stems. Best feeding practices are provided for each species.

Cryptocoryne parva *is an easy keeper that does well in low light conditions. Some low-growing plants can be quite greedy for light, so it's best to check before planting a nice lawn of tiny plants.*

SPECIAL CARE

Extra attention to lighting, feeding, substrate composition, placement in the aquarium, disease prevention, pruning or maintenance is noted here.

PROPAGATION

Most aquatic plants reproduce without any help from the gardener. Those plants that produce runners, offsets, and plantlets require no more effort than simply separating the new plant and tending to it. Many plants can be duplicated by division and cuttings as well. Those that produce seeds through sexual reproduction are more challenging, but by no means impossible, to propagate.

NOTES

There are always extra bits of advice or unusual features about individual plant species. Some plants have large root systems that need deep gravel beds to allow them to spread and support the top growth. Other species need to be trimmed frequently and the cuttings replanted in the substrate. Some do better when planted in small flowerpots with a layer of potting soil in the pot beneath the gravel. Sometimes the flower stalks should be cut rather than left to grow as a way of extending the life of the parent plant. In short, there are so many exceptions to the norm in the keeping of aquatic plants that it is nearly impossible to catalog them all. There is still much to be learned about keeping various species. These notes are intended to help you to keep different plants happy, healthy, and growing well. Over time, you are almost certain to have many notes of your own to add.

Crypts are very interesting, durable aquarium plants. This one, Cryptocoryne walkeri 'lutea', is one of the mainstays of the aquatic plant hobby.

Why aquarium plants?

An aquarium filled with live plants is an awesome sight—I've yet to meet a person who is not drawn to this captivating vision of nature. Healthy plants arranged creatively magically couple with the movements of thriving fish, making the aquarium much more than just the sum of its parts: it literally glows from within. A beautiful planted aquarium is an asset to any living or work space, and people from all walks of life and all the corners of the globe have a growing appreciation of these aquatic gardens.

Freshwater aquarium keeping divides into two schools: "plants and fish," or "fish and plants." The plants-and-fish aquarium focuses on the plants, and the few fish usually have a job to do, whether it's consuming algae or providing a little fertilizer, while adding visual interest to the aquascape. In the fish-and-plants aquarium, plants are also decorative—but they serve as well. For many fish species, being in an aquarium with live plants is as good as aquarium life gets. A heavily planted tank gives fish a sense of security. There are plants available to dart behind or into should they feel threatened. Though they may retreat to the foliage in a flash, fish in a planted tank tend to swim more in the open than fish that lack this protection. A well-planted tank means you'll see your fish more often.

Plants are also natural spawning sites for many aquarium fish. It's quite common to see egg-laying fishes like tetras and barbs cavorting in the plants, scattering eggs as they go. Adhesive eggs can be seen glittering on the fine leaves of many plants. The strong, broad leaves of the sword plants are ideal spawning sites for vertical spawners like angelfish and discus. Aquatic plants provide cover for the fry of virtually any kind of fish, protecting them from predators that would make short work of the fry in a bare aquarium. Tiny microorganisms that live on plant leaves also provide natural food for these newborns.

Healthy plants help improve water quality in your tank, too. Plants produce oxygen, consume the carbon dioxide from the fish, and assist in the reduction of organic wastes. Additionally, some

Bolbitis heudelotii has a reputation for being a bit of a challenge to get started, but if you follow a few simple steps, this impressive African fern will grow into a strong, healthy plant in your aquarium.

Cardinal Tetras, Paracheirodon axelrodi, *are well suited to the planted aquarium. The environment preferred by the tetras is suitable for growing most tropical plants.*

plants contain bactericides that help to reduce harmful bacteria in the water. But most important, plants appeal to humans. As any gardener will tell you, there is a deep satisfaction that comes with the cultivation of plants, and aquatic plants are no exception. Some of the processes for success with aquatic horticulture may be a little different, but the results are a source of pure delight.

The practice of adding live plants to aquariums can be traced back many generations. Early fish keepers had to make do without most of the equipment we have today, and they knew the value of including live plants to sweeten the water and provide a source of food and comfort for their fish. When you're keeping a few small fish in a bowl, plants are helpful even if you make daily water changes.

Without air pumps, filters, lights, or heaters, early aquarists were quite successful relying upon a wholly natural and low-tech methods of maintaining their fishes. The aquarium was lightly stocked with fish, usually one or two small cold-water species, and planted with whatever aquatic plants happened to be available locally. Partial water changes were the order of the day, but on the whole these simple, small "biotopes" were as fascinating to their owners back then as the high-tech aquariums are to modern fish keepers today.

Underwater gardening
for freshwater aquarists

The list of *needs* of aquarium plants is actually quite short. However, the list of *wants* of the aquarist is potentially very long. Fortunately, one can keep aquarium plants and fish as a hobby without a heavy wallet. Sometimes all it takes is a little imagination and a few inexpensive tools. Of course, if you have the desire and the means, the possibilities can be pretty spectacular. There are technologies (and know-how) in the hobby now that were undreamed of just a few years ago, so if you tried to keep aquarium plants in the past without success, it may just be time to try again.

Some aquatic plants are practically indestructible. Java Moss and Java Fern seem to be like that: even with low light, poor water conditions, and rough fish, their tenacity is outstanding. These plants take hold wherever they find themselves, making the best of any situation. To be sure, such highly adaptable species are the exception rather than the rule. Most of the aquatic plant species perform best when some provisions have been made for their well-being.

*The Java Fern (*Microsorum pteropus*) is among the hardiest and most forgiving of the aquatic plants. It is not bothered by herbivores, and it makes no demands as far as bright light or special fertilizers are concerned.*

Eriocaulaceae 'Type 2' is a member of the Pipewort family. These delicate-looking plants have an affinity for bright light.

HOW MUCH LIGHT IS ENOUGH?

Light is a fundamental issue in the planted aquarium. Is there enough? Is there too much? Is it the right kind? Is it reaching the plants at the bottom? And there are so many different lighting options available that it is easy to be confused. Try not to be blinded by the choices. Bright light from practically any source will promote plant growth. Some people even use sunlight. I know that's a radical concept, but aquatic plants grow extraordinarily well in vases on windowsills where the evaporated water is replaced with water being changed out of a fertile aquarium.

There are any number of ways to light an aquarium. Certainly the aquarium lighting vendors present an impressive array of options, each with its specific application. Besides the standard aquarium hood-type lighting units, creative aquarists use the light that gets the job done for the plants they are keeping. There's nothing wrong with using an 8-watt desk light to spotlight a gallon-sized planted nano tank, or a combination of room light and pendant lights to highlight sections of the aquarium.

That said, the standard "starter kit" aquarium light with incandescent bulb or bulbs is far from an optimal choice for the aquarist seeking success with aquarium plants. Incandescent bulbs are inefficient and create excessive heat that can be problematic, especially in the summer months. Instead, lighting for the planted tank is typically achieved through the use of multiple units of standard fluorescent, T5 HO (high output), VHO (very high output), compact fluorescent/power compact (PC), and metal halide/HQI lights. Aquarium lights are available in a large selection of spectrums and intensities, and also in compact sizes. T5 HO fluorescent and power compacts produce high light output in small spaces. T8 is most often used by hobbyists and offers the most options. Power compact T5, high-output T5, and metal halides are used for aquaria that need the brightest light. Bright lights suspended in luminaires over an open tank seem to offer the best of all worlds.

LIGHT INTENSITY

Unfortunately, the light produced by your unit is not necessarily the light that reaches the plants. The amount of light reaching the plants is reduced by several factors: reflection, shade, and absorption. A certain percentage of the light is reflected off the surface of the water, another part is absorbed by the light cover and minute suspended particles in the water, and still more light is lost to the bottom of the aquarium by the leaves of the plants

LIGHT LEVEL	LUX	WATTS/GALLON
Low	100–500	1–2
Medium	500–1000	2–2.5
Bright	1000–1500	2.5–3
Very Bright	1500+	3+

BULB TYPE	KELVIN	WATTS	COMMENTS
Standard Fluorescent	3,000–20,000 K	15–40	Low light plants
T5 HO	6,000–11,000 K	24–54	All light levels
VHO Fluorescent	10,000 K	75–165	All light levels
Compact Fluorescent	5,000–10,000 K	10–130	All light levels
Metal Halide	4,000–20,000 K	70–1,000	Bright light for deeper aquaria

Examples:

TANK	LIGHT LEVEL	LIGHTS
55 gallons	Low	Two 40-watt Standard Fluorescent
55 gallons	Bright	Four 40-watt Standard Fluorescent
40 gallons	Bright	Two 65-watt Power Compacts
10 gallons	Medium	24-watt T5 HO

in the upper level of the tank. With this in mind, we will make sure that we eliminate factors that might further reduce the light reaching the bottom: by cleaning the light covers regularly, keeping an eye on the density of plants at the surface, and making sure the water is kept clear of suspended particulate matter by good mechanical filtration. Light penetration is usually not a major problem in the relatively shallow home aquarium, but light intensity becomes markedly reduced at depths of over 3 feet. Also, it is often the nature of the smaller plants that hug the substrate to require less intense light than others because they would likely also be shaded by bigger plants in their native environments.

Most aquarists measure their lighting intensity in watts per gallon. Simply add up the total wattage of the bulbs over the tank and divide by the number of gallons. For planted tanks, 2 to 3 watts per gallon is generally adequate. With very deep tanks and plants that require bright light, as much as 4 or 5 watts per gallon could be necessary. Lux represents the amount of light provided. The table (at left) gives light levels in terms of lux and watts to achieve different lighting levels.

The lighting levels recommended for the plant species—bright, medium, or low—are best for those species. But plants live in a range of conditions, so a plant that prefers low light could be very stable in a bright aquarium with 3 to 5 watts reaching the gravel if it was shaded by a piece of driftwood or lived in the shadow of a larger plant. Use bright light unless you are specifically designing a low-light aquascape. Many of the nicest foreground plants need bright

Rotala wallichii is demanding: it needs plenty of light and very soft water, and it benefits from the use of CO_2 and extra attention to fertilization. For this little bit of extra trouble, this delicate-looking plant will present with deep red growing tips, a hit with the aquarium designers.

21

Blyxa japonica forms a soft, green lawn in bright, well-fertilized aquaria. It propagates via runners.

light, so if you like the look of a grassy plain across the front glass of the tank, use wattages that will penetrate the depth.

A lamp produces light of certain colors, or wavelengths. Each type of lamp, depending upon the material from which it is constructed, will emit red, yellow, green, and blue in different intensities. For photosynthetic purposes plants favor the warm red and orange over the yellow and green, and pick up power again on the blue-green end of the spectrum. Both blue-green and orange-red wavelengths are necessary for healthy plants.

The color spectrum of light is noted as a "Kelvin rating." Natural sunlight gives a reading of 6,500 K. Most plant enthusiasts look for bulbs in the 5,000 K to 10,000 K range. Full-spectrum lighting in the area of 6,500 K is ideal for plant growth and viewing pleasure. There are special plant bulbs that produce light in the red and blue areas of the color spectrum, which focuses on the colors of light that plants use most, and these are also excellent. Avoid the use of "cool white" utility bulbs or ultra-blue "reef aquarium" tubes used by marine aquarists, which may have ratings as high as 20,000 K.

Generally, light green plants require the brightest light; dark green plants accept lower light; and red-hued plants reflect red light and use light from the blue end of the spectrum.

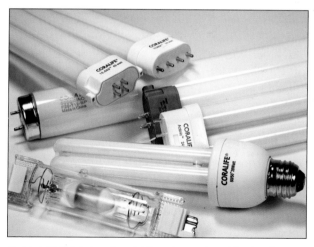

Aquarium lighting choices abound: full-spectrum and specialty plant fluores-cents are most popular, while T5, compact fluorescents, and metal halide bulbs provide higher-intensity lighting for deeper tanks and demanding plants.

Power compact fixtures now offer an affordable method of bringing bright light to planted aquariums without the heat and expense of metal halides.

LIGHTING OPTIONS

Fluorescent lights provide great value for the money spent. They are cool-running and will not overheat the water. Many aquarists report good results with "full spectrum," "daylight," and specialty "aquarium plant" lights—available from every aquarium shop, garden center, and good hardware store that caters to gardeners.

High color-performance fluorescent tubes will give you the color and intensity of light you need. Usually about 2 watts per gallon is sufficient, but if CO_2 is added to the water, the light intensity needs to be adjusted upward to correspond to increased plant growth.

Keep in mind that fluorescent bulbs age, shift spectrum, and lose intensity over time. Fluorescent bulbs should be changed every 6 to 12 months (try to have the bulbs on a rotating schedule; i.e., a new bulb every 6 months rather than two new bulbs every year).

Metal halide fixtures and high-output and power compact lighting. Most aquarists use fluorescent lighting, but the good light work that has been done on the marine side of the hobby has made many high-quality metal halide fixtures and high-output and power compact lighting available. These are most important to people who have large, deep tanks and are prepared to invest in higher-tech equipment. When the planted aquarium is high art, and the goal is maximum growth in the short term—perhaps for the length of time it takes to ready for a competition or to get one perfect photo—there are many high-quality systems and much detailed information available via the planted aquarium societies and clubs.

SUNLIGHT

Natural sunlight would be great for the plants in the aquarium if we could count on it. The changing seasons have a lot to do with how much sunlight the aquarium will receive, though, and the tank that gets good light in the spring might well turn into an algae-ridden hot tub in the middle of the summer. If you are going to supplement your artificial lighting with the free light that streams through your windows, be sure you plan your location carefully. The best arrangement would be to place the tank a few feet from a window in an area that receives morning light. Be sure you can "turn off the light" with a curtain or shade if the water has a tendency to overheat or if you find that algae is taking over.

LIGHTING DURATION

Tropical plants require 12 hours of light a day, every day. However, you can't make up for low-intensity light or light of the wrong spectrum by increasing the duration of the lighting. The duration of light is much more important than most people realize. Even if the lighting intensity is adequate, the plants cannot produce enough energy to live if the lights are not left on long enough. Twelve hours each day is ideal; less than 10 or more than 14 is not advised.

Because the duration of light is so important to aquatic plants, one of the most inexpensive but useful accessories you can ever buy for your aquarium is a timer for the lights. Day-in and day-out predictability of photoperiod is important to both plants and fishes.

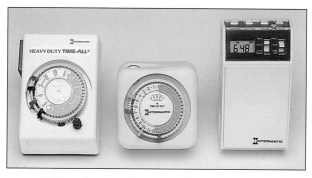

An essential piece of equipment for every aquarium is a lighting timer, establishing a stable photoperiod for the benefit of both plants and fishes.

CONDITIONS TO MAKE PLANTS THRIVE

The water in which you keep your aquatic plants is just as important to them as it is to your fish. Fish keepers are attuned to the temperature, pH, and hardness requirements of fish, but often they don't think of those things when considering plants. As you learn more about the different plant species, it will become apparent that they, too, have preferences with regard to the water conditions. The water that comes from your tap is less than ideal for the various species. If your water contains chlorine or chloramines, you must use the appropriate water conditioners to remove those harmful substances. Reverse osmosis units can purify virtually any tap-water problem. Sometimes tap water is too hard and alkaline for the rainforest species that thrive in soft, acidic water. Water chemistry can be altered to suit the preferences of various plants, of course, but my best advice to most hobbyists is to grow the plants that thrive in the water that suits your fish. Test your water chemistry, so that you at least have an idea of the pH and hardness of your source water. Doing so will save you money and grief over lost plants and fish.

Many aquatic plants are actually grown emersed, or out of water, at the aquatic nursery. When they are planted in the aquarium, it can take them some time to adjust to submersed life.

Your water can be hardened easily by the addition of benign chemicals with a water hardness test kit as your guide. Softening water is a little more difficult. Some serious hobbyists (or people who have very unhospitable water) run the source water through water softening resins or reverse-osmosis membranes, adding back in necessary trace elements. Really serious hobbyists collect rainwater and use that mixed with aged tap water to refill their tanks. There is much to know about water chemistry, but most of us do not need the information. If plants grow for us, they grow for us, and little further attention to water chemistry is required other than to keep an eye on the pH and make sure the ammonia doesn't rise.

pH

pH is a measurement of how acidic or alkaline the water is. It is measured by test kit or pH pen or monitor with a probe. Most tropical plants favor a pH slightly below 7, which is neutral. There are some species that flourish in hard water with alkaline pH, and they are noted among the plant species. There are even some plants that

This is a pair of Dwarf Gouramis, Colisa lalia. These fish are perfect in the conditions favored by most aquatic plants in the aquarium.

thrive in brackish and marine waters, but these are the exception. The pH tends to decrease over time, meaning that aquarium water acidity increases, so it is important to test it, frequently at first, and then, once you have a good sense of how much it drops and why, test at water changes.

Monitoring the pH in a planted tank will give a clear picture of the health of the system. Excessive feeding and waste material in

Hemigrammus bleheri, the Rummy-Nosed Tetra, is an ideal schooling species for planted aquaria. In addition to being very attractive, this fish's bright red snout loses color when the water chemistry becomes unsuitable, making it a perfect barometer of the health of the aquarium.

the tank will cause the pH to drop, sometimes dangerously so. Sharp drops in pH are indicative of the need for attention in the form of water changes or possibly increased carbonate hardness (kH). In tanks treated to CO_2 injection, pH monitoring is essential. Peat filtration, driftwood, acid buffers, biological filtration, and CO_2 injection lower pH; alkaline buffers, use of limestone or coral substrate, and aeration (which reduces CO_2 levels in the water) raise pH.

WATER HARDNESS

Water hardness is a measurement of the dissolved elements in the water. Mostly, it is comprised of calcium and magnesium salts and trace elements. Alkalinity (carbonate hardness) is kH, or temporary hardness. Permanent hardness is a measurement of other dissolved elements such as nitrates, sulfides, and so on. The sum of kH and permanent hardness is general hardness, or gH.

Water that has low carbonate hardness, or alkalinity, is subject to unstable pH levels. The alkalinity produces the "buffering capacity" that stabilizes the pH, and when necessary, is increased by adding carbonate to the water. Low kH is unsuitable in any aquarium, as the swinging pH levels will undermine your efforts to maintain a healthy aquarium. Baking soda (sodium bicarbonate) and commercially available buffering products will raise the kH and help stabilize pH.

Any changes to the water in the aquarium, whether it is temperature or water chemistry, must be performed gradually. Aquarium plants and fish do well in a range of conditions, but even changes within the range for the species will stress the organisms if the changes occur suddenly. When altering the water chemistry in any way, whether it is to lower the pH or to add nutrients, it is prudent to mix the amendments to replacement water in containers separate from the aquarium, test the mix, and then add that water to the aquarium. Adding chemicals straight to the tank can be a recipe for disaster, and one accident can mean the difference between success and failure.

WATER HARDNESS CHART

DESCRIPTION	CaCO$_3$	GH
Very Soft	0–70 ppm	0–4
Soft	71–140 ppm	5–8
Medium Hard	141–320 ppm	9–18
Hard	over 321 ppm	over 18

Note: ppm = mg/l
One gH = 17.8 ppm CaCO$_3$

SETTING UP THE TANK

Once you have your aquarium and a stand for it, you will want to choose the best location. The tank stand should be sturdy, and the aquarium should not be placed in the busiest area of the house, both for the sake of the fishes and for the safety of the tank. Some plant people like to place the aquarium where it will get a modest dose of sunlight every day. This is fine, but don't forget that the weather is totally beyond our control. If you do elect to place the aquarium where it will get the free light of the sun, be sure that there is a window shade or curtain to limit the bounty if necessary.

FILTRATION

Filtration is desirable, of course, to house and nourish nitrifying bacteria, mechanically filter wastes, to keep the water clear, and even to create some current. Filters that create surface turbulence are shunned by most aquatic gardeners, as the desire is generally to keep the surface of the water calm. By the same token, airstones are best kept for tanks where the fish load demands additional oxygen. A small inside power filter is usually all that is required for the aver-

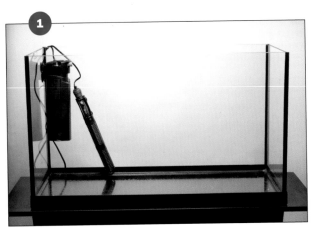

Modern rimless aquaria are especially decorative to use with aquatic plants. The inside power filter and heater will disappear in the finished aquarium design. Place the power filter low in the tank so the surface tension of the water is undisturbed, yet there is water movement below the surface to move the gasses around.

Use a rinsed substrate, optimally mixed with a portion of the substrate from a healthy, mature aquarium. If this is an all-new setup, consider fertilizing the substrate before heavily planting the aquarium. This will considerably reduce the time it takes for this aquarium to cycle and become stable both chemically and biologically.

Carefully place your hardscape (the rocks, bogwood, and any other design elements) into the aquarium before adding water or plants. This way, you can move everything around until it looks right without damaging the tender, new plants. Be sure to place any fertilizers you wish to use into the substrate at this time.

Fill the aquarium about one-third to one-half the depth with aged water that you bring up to temperature, and correct the water chemistry before you add your plants or fishes. The slight cloudiness will clear when you turn on the filter, which should be allowed to run for at least 24 hours before adding livestock of any kind.

When first planting the tank, do so fully with fast-growing bunch plants for the least troublesome "break-in" period. In time, you can add your "wish list" plants and share the excess stemmed plant growth with fellow hobbyists, start more aquaria, or even trade it back to your local fish shop. The key is to have the plants working in the tank from the very start.

Once you have all the plants placed securely in the substrate (sometimes this requires the help of a judiciously placed rock), gently fill the aquarium with more aged, treated water. Even if your tap water is perfect without adjustments (and I hope it is!), letting it stand for at least 24 hours is a golden practice to develop in aquarium husbandry.

Left: All equipment is concealed in the cabinet below this 33-gallon full working aquarium.

In as little as six weeks, the filter is fine, and the plants have filled in. A few fishes add color and movement to the growing scenery.

Roots, beautiful roots! Don't underestimate the power of the roots of your plants. Many times, those roots hidden away under the substrate are as large as the plant you see above the gravel.

age planted aquarium. For larger systems, an outside canister filter or fluidized bed filter with the outflow positioned so the water return is below the surface is ideal.

SUBSTRATE

Gravel is the usual choice for the substrate in the aquarium. The substrate most often recommended for the planted aquarium is clean washed gravel with grains of 1/12 inch (3 mm) in diameter.

Many people who keep aquatic plants like to experiment with substrates. They use many things, from leaf mold to cow manure, to enrich the substrate for the benefit of their plants. While it may seem like a good idea, this path is perilous for the inexperienced, and I do not recommend it on a wholesale basis. For the most part, unless you are heavily into experimentation and don't mind losing your plants and fish, stay away from products that have not been proven safe in the aquarium. There are any number of nutrient-enriched substrates on the market, and they all have their advocates. Fertilizer can be added to the substrate or to the water column. Liquid fertilizers need to be used fairly frequently, but substrate fertilizers generally last for months. Heater cables are sometimes used under the gravel to promote biological activity within the substrate.

The substrate should be deep, 3 inches or more. If the substrate is too shallow, the plants will escape and float around the tank. There must be enough gravel for the roots to take hold and spread. You will find that some of your show specimens, such as the sword plants, have large root systems. For these, you must supply adequate depth so that the roots do not work their way out of the gravel. If you attempt to anchor these roots in shallow gravel, it is likely that the roots will be damaged, as they must be repeatedly replaced into the substrate.

The substrate should remain undisturbed after the plants have been inserted. If you are planting in sand or gravel only, you will disturb the roots. If you are using layers of even finer substrates—laterite, clay, vermiculite, and the like—as many hobbyists do—you will have an unholy mess.

LATERITE

Laterite is one of the many substrate materials that have become popular in recent years. It is very rich in iron and will release small amounts into the water, which helps to nourish the plants and helps to prevent chlorosis, an abnormal condition of plants that shows up as a lack of green pigment; it is caused by light deprivation, iron or mineral deficiency, or genetic disorders. A very reliable way of telling when the iron concentration is low (besides using a commercial test kit) is when the green plants change shade, losing their dark green hue and turning pale.

Laterite is best used during the initial setup of a new tank. It is not practical to try to add laterite to an existing tank, because it must be used under the substrate unless you want a mess of laterite dust clouding up the water ever after. The recommended procedure is to mix 25 percent laterite with 75 percent gravel to form a bed about 1 inch deep on the entire floor of the tank. Then top this mix with your other substrate materials.

While collecting your own specimens is a wonderful offshoot of the hobby, take care in strange waters. I just know there are alligators in that puddle!

The world of aquatic plants: where to start?

You may be ready to establish a brand-new tank dedicated to plants or you may want to start adding plants to an existing aquarium. The methods are a bit different, but the end result of a beautifully aquascaped tank is possible no matter where you are in the process. A new tank offers endless possibilities for decorating with aquarium plants. With a little thought, you can create virtually any underwater scene you desire. You can approximate the natural environment of a select fish species or group of species with their native plants and other aquatic features like rocks and driftwood or dry areas and waterfalls.

Aquariums can be as natural or as imaginative as you wish within the bounds of good aquarium practice. Some people like the micro-environment and thrill to the fact that they can keep an eco-logically sound 1-gallon container as a living diorama; others relish the artistic expression of the Zen aquarium; then there are those who

This colorful collection of aquarium plants is part of a mail-order shipment. Buying aquatic plants through the mail is a good way to acquire the more unusual and specialized species. Plants ship very well and the few mishaps are generally replaced by reputable vendors.

This aquarium was set up in just a few hours as a display for a planted aquarium society at an aquatics convention in the U.K.

just want to live in the tropics with a house full of lagoon-size planted tanks, orchids, and screaming parrots. (Maybe monkeys, too.)

FINDING STOCK

Tropical plants are highly prized in the aquarium, but don't be surprised to discover that many of the most clever and attractive of tanks are filled with native species. One nation's nuisance plant is often the whole rage in aquarium specimens. While most of the plants we keep in the aquarium are mass-grown in nurseries, the really new species are collected from the wild by botanists and hobbyists, both professional and amateur.

When you are shopping for aquarium plants, take a good hard look at the stock. You want plants that have been kept in well-lit tanks. If the plant section is a small, dark aquarium with a few limp-looking specimens, buy your plants elsewhere.

If you can find a shop that caters to planted-tank enthusiasts, you have found a treasure. Build a relationship with the personnel and let them know what you are looking for. If they have good plants,

Fissidens fontanus *is native to the U.S. and is proving to be both malleable and useful in the aquarium. It makes no special demands and is simple to keep.*

they have a good supplier, and will be able to special-order the plants you want as they show up on the wholesaler's offering list. This is key, as good aquarium plants are not always easy to find. Very few people can make a list of species they want and expect to find them in one trip. Patience is more than a virtue; it is essential if you are going to find the plants you want. The availability of various species is often seasonal, with more plants ready for market at certain times of the year. Take advantage of this and buy what you need whenever you find it.

If you are having trouble sourcing your plants locally (a problem in more rural areas), there are many mail-order suppliers specializing in aquatic plants. They are often the source of amazing selections.

WHAT TO LOOK FOR

While full-grown specimens command premium prices, even on budget you shouldn't have to settle for a plant that is barely alive. Look for young plants with crisp white roots and healthy top growth. If you see new growth, it's a good sign that even a small

The diminutive Glossostigma elatinoides. *This photo shows how a thick rug of Glosso forms with a support of craft mesh on the substrate.*

Remove the plastic pots prior to planting. If you let the roots grow through them indefinitely, they will be damaged when you remove the pot later.

plant will do well. The roots are more important at this stage than the top growth. Plants with a healthy root system should be able to establish well in the aquarium and get on with the business of producing new leaves.

Potted plants come with their own little plastic pots and pumice wool impregnated with fertilizer that will last for about three months. This is an excellent way to buy plants. The potted plants are grown hydroponically; that is, without soil, in the inert medium. The fertilizer-impregnated fibrous substrate serves to protect the tender young roots and it will not change the pH or water chemistry. A large plant will grow out of the small pot. For group plantings, remove the pot but retain the supplied substrate for its fertilizer.

Treat strange plants as if they are carrying unwanted snail eggs or parasites. Once when I floated some new plants in a tank, I was alerted by wild activity of the fishes. A caterpillar had come in with the plants, and the fishes were thrilled! If you don't want to risk introducing strange organisms into your tank, it helps to dip them in a weak solution of potassium permanganate (use just enough to turn the water light pink) and rinse well. It's not unheard of for people with a large stake in the hobby to quarantine plants as they would fishes.

While you are still in the "thinking stage" of this project, consider these points: All the plants you choose should have about the same needs with regard to light, temperature, and water conditions. Use contrasting shapes and colors to create an aesthetically pleasing effect. Don't forget to include open space. You may be able to grow big, healthy plants, but if they are too crowded you'll barely be able to tell where one begins and the other leaves off. The size of the tank is a limiting factor. Some aquatic plants, like many *Echinodorus* (sword plants), can get very big. Some sword plants are so vigorous that they will grow up and out of the tank, flowering profusely. In a 70-gallon tank the effect can be lovely, especially if you actively tried to achieve it; in a 10-gallon tank, you might feel that you need to call a plant exterminator.

PLANTING POINTERS

When the aquarium is ready for the plants, you can bring home your purchases. Keep the plants warm and moist during the trip home. If the specimens get chilled or dry out, their chances for survival are severely reduced. Trim off damaged leaves, stems, and

Snails are usually looked upon askance in the aquarium, but the Malaysian Trumpet Snail comes in very handy in "roto-rootering" the substrate, something that we cannot do too vigorously without disturbing the aquarium.

43

roots. They will not "come back" and will only rot in your water and clog your filter.

It is best to use hardy plants in the beginning with any aquarium: *Sagittaria*, *Riccia*, Water Sprite, and the two Javas, Fern and Moss, are very forgiving while we are fine-tuning our methods and practices. Plant them with a free hand; then, as the system stabilizes and you begin to see new growth, make room for the more demanding species.

Planting abundantly right from the start in a new tank will prevent algae blooms and perhaps even prevent other water-quality problems. Heavy plantings provide a safety margin to any new fresh-water aquarium, and the fish should be added slowly after the plants have been given a week or two to get established. This gives the filtration and biological processes time to start up. An exception to this is made for the useful little suckermouth catfish *Otocinclus*. These algae-loving fish will help to prevent algae films from ever starting in the tank and will amuse you with their industrious grazing.

When keeping challenging plants, or those that are questionable with regard to keeping protocols, by all means pot them up. Moving them to "better" quarters will be much less traumatic if you haven't uprooted the plant for the move.

The roots on this Crinum calamistratum *are growing from a small bulb. They are in good shape to take on the job of nourishing the plant. This species consumes a fair amount of phosphorus. Within a few weeks, this plant anchored in the substrate with finer roots and the new leaves grew vigorously.*

These delicate crypts flower in the protection of the flowerpot. Anytime you want to give a special plant extra attention or limit its expansion through your aquarium, pot it up.

10 BEST PLANTS FOR BEGINNERS

Starting with sure winners makes great sense for the newcomer to aquarium keeping. There are good reasons why so many hobbyists start with Zebra Danio and *Corydoras* Catfishes—they are survivors. The same holds true with aquarium plants. If in doubt, here are 10 of the Most Likely Succeed (to give you the confidence to move on to more challenging species).

- **Anubias** (*Anubias* spp.)
- **Colorata Rotala** (*Rotala* sp. 'Colorata')
- **Downoi** (*Pogostemon helferi*)
- **Dwarf Sag** (*Sagittaria subulata*)
- **Fissidens** (*Fissidens fontanus*)
- **Java Fern** (*Microsorum* spp.)
- **Java Moss** (*Vesicularia* spp.)
- **Jungle Val** (*Vallisneria spiralis*)
- **Riccia** (*Riccia fluitans*)
- **Water Sprite** (*Ceratopteris thalictroides*)

Limnophila aromatica is a most effective stem plant for aquascaping, showing up brilliantly against bright green plants, especially those that form a carpet.

ABOUT THE PLANTS

The term "bunch" as it applies to stemmed aquatic plants has more to do with how they are usually sold than any habits of their own. They are bunched together, half a dozen or so pieces, and it's up to you to separate and root them and get them going in the home aquarium. They can and will root in time with proper care, but it can be challenging to get them to stay put so they don't float around the tank. Once they do take hold, they are likely to get so long that they'll curl around the top of the tank. Anacharis (*Elodea*) is probably the most commonly sold bunch-type plant.

Bunch plants most often reproduce by cuttings (which is how they themselves are generally supplied), but when they flower, they could produce seeds as well. Bunches must be separated and prepared for planting. Unwrap the lead weight and discard; it is not meant for permanent use in your tank.

When planting, cut off the bottoms of the stems and remove the lower leaves. Plant in small, loose clusters of about three stems (odd numbers seem to work better) with about the width of the bunch between each group. Gently plant a group of 4- to 6-inch stems in fine gravel where it won't be disturbed. When you see new top growth, you know you have done well. It never hurts to secure your bunches with a ring of stones or other bit of hardscape until the roots hold the plant in place on their own.

Rooted plants enjoy a bit more status than the simple cuttings offered in bunches, and their price tags reflect the same. The rooted plants are sold either in small perforated plastic pots with an artificial substrate of fertilizer-impregnated pumice fibers or bare-rooted. Some rooted plants, with rhizomes that form rootlets, are sold with their roots anchored to gravel or a bit of wood.

The chances for having the potted plants do well in the aquarium are much greater than those of the bare-root plants, provided they have not been abused in transit. Plants will grow new leaves readily, but if the roots are badly damaged, it can take a long time for a plant to recover. With any plant that has had a tough trip, I like to float it in a healthy, fertile tank until I see new growth. Don't bury potential problems. Snip off rotting leaves and roots, and plant the specimen when new growth appears. For tiny plants that need special attention to get started, float the plants in a small container with fresh tank water. Rooted plants like *Sagittaria, Vallisneria*, and *Ceratopteris* should all have their roots buried and the crowns above the surface of the gravel. If the crowns are buried, the plant will rot.

Roots grow from the rhizomes of plants like Anubias. *The rhizomes attach to ridged or uneven surfaces like stones, driftwood, or bark, with tiny rootlets that, once established, have amazing tenacity.*

Rhizomes are a type of modified root that serve as a nutrient depot, a lateral shoot-producing organ, and maker of holdfasts for the plant. Generally, rhizomes should not be planted in the substrate but instead attached to a surface where they can gain a foothold. Plants with rhizomes, such as *Anubias, Bolbitis,* and *Cryptocoryne,* should be planted shallowly. Their roots should be covered, and the rhizome should be just below the surface of the gravel.

To propagate from a rhizome root, sever the rhizome with a sharp blade at the new-growth end.

Bulb plants, like *Crinum* spp., *Barclaya* spp., *Aponogeton* spp., and others, are easily planted. Just be sure not to cover the bulb completely. In time, the plant will set strong roots that will anchor the bulb in the substrate. Some bulb plants develop tiny bulblets at the base of the bulb. These can be severed with a sharp instrument when they start to become crowded. Plant them separately.

Floating plants, like *Limnobium laevigatum* (Frogbit), *Riccia,* and many others, are charming and generally easy to keep. As floating plants, they generally have first crack at the light, though, and this could be a problem for plants growing beneath, which may quickly become starved for light. Other than this, floating plants are useful and enjoyable to see in an aquarium. They serve to calm nervous fishes and seem to reduce jumping. They're very good for fry tanks, where they offer cover, nourishment, and improved water quality.

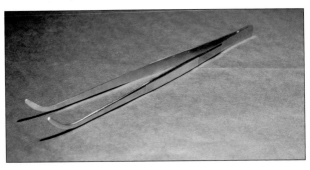

Gardening instruments, like tissue scissors, tweezers, and forceps, are all very helpful in maintaining the planted aquarium. There will be a lot of trimming and pruning to keep the tank looking its best. Be sure tools have long handles. This goes a long way toward keeping your sleeves dry.

Some plants, such as this water lily, will grow emersed and flower when the aquarium has an open area at the top.

Depending on the type of tank you're keeping, floating plants may be just the thing. Some floating plants, like *Riccia*, can be temporarily anchored to substrate with cotton thread or a hairnet. It's best to use a living substrate like Java Moss that has anchored to the hardscape. *Riccia* will form a thick mat over the Java Moss, which will continue to grow with interesting and attractive results.

DECORATING WITH PLANTS

Certain combinations of plants, fish, and accessories are just natural together. Angelfish, *Vallisneria spiralis*, and *Echinodorus quadricostatus* equal simple perfection. A tank full of Water Sprite (*Ceratopteris thalictroides*) and fancy guppies is both decorative and functional, as the fine leaves of the plant offer protection to successive generations of colorful guppies.

The configuration you use to place plants when planning and planting the decorative aquarium is very important to the "eye appeal" of the finished project. The placement of different groups of plants is based on various compositional shapes, triangles, semicircles, and so on, but rarely on straight lines. The shapes and sizes of some individual plants lend themselves to certain placement within the aquarium.

Start with the background plants. These are usually long-stemmed and tall. The background material should not be notice-

One of the new stars in the constellation of aquatic plants. Known as "Downoi," or "Little Star," *Pogostemon helferi is in high demand throughout the world as word spreads of this distinctive and versatile aquarium discovery.*

able enough to overpower the planting at the back of the aquarium. Background plants are usually the ones that require the most light, the red-leafed plants like *Alternanthera reineckii* or *Rotala wallichii*. When arranging your background plants, bring them around the sides of the tank as well.

Foreground plants are typically short, dense plants such as *Cryptocoryne wendtii*, *Anubias barteri* var. *nana*, *Sagittaria subulata*, and *Echinodorus tenellus*. These are usually planted generously and permitted in time to cover the entire available substrate with growth.

Specimen plants. Off to the right or left of the center of the tank, specimen plants like *Echinodorus amazonicus* share the stage with driftwood or rock formations.

For many aquarists, the more varieties of plants used, the more interesting and appealing the planted tank. Others prefer to have limited numbers of species grown in masses. Some stunning tanks use just a single type of plant. A very attractive tank can be created with nothing more than a piece of driftwood and Java Fern. This is ideal when the fish of your choice are noted for digging up or eating plants. The Java Fern can be attached to the driftwood with fishing line or thread and will grow to cover the wood (or even rocks) in no time at all.

This lush aquarium is very low-tech. Its owner just calls it "weeds."

Christmas Tree Moss is an enchanting newcomer to the aquatic-plant hobby. Not only is it a great tank tenant, but the potential for metaphor in planted aquarium design is priceless.

Rotala verticillaris is a delightful new Australian plant that will surely enjoy many fans in times to come.

A field guide to aquarium plants: species that can thrive for you

For the aquatic plant enthusiast, bringing home a new plant—one whose native habitat might be at the foot of a tropical waterfall in the South Pacific, a rice paddy in Asia, a remote stream in West Africa, or a jungle pool in the upper reaches of the Amazon basin—is one of life's pulse-quickening moments.

To know that you are not bringing home a plant that can't possibly survive in your aquarium is elevating. No one wants to have their aquarium dreams trashed when the beautiful plants that comprise the scene melt before your very eyes. The following 101 species are presented are all great choices, especially for less-experienced aquatic gardeners, and include the information you need to have in order to select the right plants for your particular aquarium setup.

COLOR KEY TO PLACEMENT

One of the most important criteria for the selection of a plant is where it will eventually thrive in the aquarium. Will it fit in your aquarium? Maximum size is adequate to know the height of a plant, but spread counts as well in the overall size of the plant. The Placement Key will help you decide where to place plants in the aquascape.

Here is the Placement Key used in this guide:

FOREGROUND PLANT: Low-growing plants that carpet the substrate beneath open swimming areas in the aquarium.

MIDGROUND OR SMALL SPECIMEN PLANT: Medium-sized plants that fill between foreground and background plants.

BACKGROUND OR LARGE SPECIMEN PLANT: Largest plants in height and/or width that look best along the back and sides of the aquarium.

Ram-Angels, pretty unusual, and probably hybrids, but obviously happy and healthy in their beautiful aquatic garden.

Alternanthera reineckii
Telanthera, Rosaefolia

OVERVIEW: Telanthera is a desirable plant that manifests in lovely shades of green, purple, red, and pink. It is commercially available with varietal names descriptive of these colors. 'Pink', or 'Rosaefolia', is said to be the easiest variety to grow.

HABITAT: Rivers, lakes, swamps; occasionally terrestrial.

NATIVE RANGE: South America.

MAXIMUM HEIGHT: 20 in. (50 cm).

LIGHTING: Bright.

WATER: 75–80°F (24–27°C); pH: slightly acidic; hardness: soft to moderately hard.

FEEDING: This plant benefits from a fine, fertile substrate with nitrogen and phosphorus fertilization. It does very well with supplemental CO_2; however, it will grow fine without CO_2 injection.

SPECIAL CARE: Strong lighting is the key to maintaining this wonderful midground plant, without which it loses color, and the leaves rot as the stems lengthen to reach for the light. Follow the caveats about light and food. Do not crowd Telanthera; it requires elbow room and gentle water circulation to achieve its full potential.

PROPAGATION: Stem cuttings rooted in substrate. Using stems that already have nodal roots increases the success rate. Can also be grown from seed.

NOTES: Roots form on the stem nodes to absorb nutrients from the water. Do not remove these roots; they are working parts, bringing nutrients directly from the water to every plant part. Pruning tips encourages bushy growth.

Ammannia gracilis
Red Ammannia

OVERVIEW: Red Ammannia is a great plant for color contrast. A group of several stems planted midground will soon form a bushy backdrop for a shorter carpet of lighter green foreground plants.

HABITAT: Marshes, streams, and riverbanks.

NATIVE RANGE: West Africa.

MAXIMUM HEIGHT: 20 in. (50 cm).

LIGHTING: Requires strong lighting to maintain bronze coloration.

WATER: 72–82°F (22–28°C); pH: mildly acidic; hardness: moderately soft.

FEEDING: Supplement iron and macronutrients; CO_2 injection desirable.

SPECIAL CARE: Delicate leaves grow quite quickly when provided with a nutrient-rich loose substrate, gentle water circulation, and adequate feeding. Low nitrate promotes the desirable reddish coloration.

PROPAGATION: Stem cuttings and side shoots. When emersed, this plant produces a small lilac flower, but propagation from seed is difficult.

NOTES: If not given strong enough light, the plant will lose its lower leaves, growth will decrease, and remaining leaves will be pale and sickly. Take care when planting not to put all the stems into one hole. Plant each stem adjacent to the others but in individual holes. This will help ensure that the lower leaves are not deprived of light and water circulation. Emersed plants are tougher and hardier than the delicate submersed form.

Anubias barteri* var. *nana
Anubias

OVERVIEW: The genus *Anubias* contains several popular species and varieties. *A. barteri*, with its varieties *barteri*, *caladifolia*, and *nana*, and *A. angustifolia* 'Afzelii' are but a few of the common anubias. There are variations in size and leaf shape and appearance, but keeping practices are similar.

HABITAT: Marshes, streams, and riverbanks, often shady.

NATIVE RANGE: West Africa.

MAXIMUM HEIGHT: 12 in. (30 cm).

LIGHTING: Low to moderate lighting.

WATER: 72–82°F (22–26°C); pH: acidic to alkaline; hardness: soft to moderately hard.

SPECIAL CARE: These perennials are so slow-growing, the leaves may acquire a coat of algae if kept in an overly fertilized environment.

PROPAGATION: Side shoots or rhizome. Seed.

NOTES: Anubias are amphibious, broad-leaved plants. The roots form on a creeping rhizome. In aquariums, these plants grow best when the rhizome is attached to rocks, driftwood, or other decorative substrate. Burying the roots and rhizome in substrate is not recommended. Because of its thick, leathery leaves, the slow-growing Anubias is ideal for aquaria with cichlids and other fishes that would not otherwise be candidates for a planted aquarium. As long as the rhizome is kept moist and the air humid, these plants will grow and sometimes flower above the waterline, which makes them interesting paludarium specimens. In good light, new leaves are initially pale in color.

Anubias barteri 'Marble Leaf'

Anubias barteri var. *nana* 'Petite'

Anubias barteri 'Broad Leaf'

Anubias barteri 'Coffeefolia'

Anubias barteri var. *nana* 'Eyes'

Anubias barteri var. *nana* 'Gold'

Anubias barteri var. *nana*
'Wrinkled Leaf'

Anubias sp. 'Garbon'

ANUBIAS • LOW LIGHT • EASY

Aponogeton boivinianus
Boivinianus

OVERVIEW: Boivinianus is a splendid but somewhat difficult speci-men plant for a large aquarium. Its full seersucker-rippled leaves make it one of the most beautiful of the _Aponogetons_.

HABITAT: Rivers and streams with strong currents.

NATIVE RANGE: Madagascar and outlying islands.

MAXIMUM HEIGHT: 24 in. (60 cm).

LIGHTING: Bright light is best. At lower levels of light intensity, the plant's leaves will be stunted.

WATER: 68–79°F (20–26°C); pH: mildly acidic to mildly alkaline; hardness: soft to moderately hard.

FEEDING: Add nutrients to the substrate, and CO_2 fertilization to the aquarium.

SPECIAL CARE: Make sure there is good current in the aquarium. Because this plant is found in moving water, experts agree that the current is one of the requirements for this species' success. Place Boivinianus near a powerhead or filter outflow.

PROPAGATION: From seed or pollination.

NOTES: Boivinianus is not abundant even in the wild, and it takes some dedication to keep it long-term in captivity. Do not use a tightly packed substrate—loose with good water circulation around the roots and through the leaves is best.

Boivinianus requires a dormant period, though the timing is unpredictable, starting spontaneously and ending the same way. When dormancy begins, reduce the light and lower the temperature. The tuber can be stored in damp moss in a temperate environment.

Aponogeton crispus
Crispus, Ruffled Sword Plant

OVERVIEW: While the leaves of Boivinianus are compared to seersucker, the leaf edges of the large and elegant Crispus are curled and ruffled. Crispus occurs in both green and brown forms. Another variety of this plant, *A. crispus* 'Kompakt', is cultured, and as the name suggests, it is a more compact form. Crispus grows rapidly in bright light and fertile substrate.

HABITAT: Quiet and running water in lakes and ponds that dry up periodically.

NATIVE RANGE: Southeast Asia.

MAXIMUM HEIGHT: 20 in. (50 cm).

LIGHTING: Bright light preferred but will tolerate less.

WATER: 72–86°F (22–30°C); pH: slightly acid; hardness: soft to slightly hard.

FEEDING: Crispus grows best with a fertile substrate.

SPECIAL CARE: No special care required.

PROPAGATION: From seed or pollination. Flowers often.

NOTES: *Aponogeton crispus* is one of the species that is sold as a "wonder bulb." It's a fast grower that works hard to enhance the aquarium even when all the conditions are not quite perfect. If the light is scant, it simply grows longer stems so the leaves can reach the surface in search of light. Bulbs start to produce leaves even if they are not planted in the substrate immediately, and young plants are easy to raise. Crispus produces one scented flower spike that is self-fertile. Cutting the flower will not prevent dormancy, though a dormant period is not required in the aquarium.

Aponogeton longiplumulosus
Longiplumulosus

OVERVIEW: Longiplumulosus is a slim, elegant plant well suited as a specimen or background plant. Its long, slender, ruffled leaves grow out of a long tuber and are quite fragile and slightly transparent. A large plant, Longiplumulosus is best suited to larger aquariums.

HABITAT: Permanent bodies of moving water.

NATIVE RANGE: Northern Madagascar.

MAXIMUM HEIGHT: 24 in. (60 cm).

LIGHTING: Very bright light is best, but it will tolerate bright light.

WATER: 71–79°F (22–26°C); pH: acid to neutral; hardness: soft to moderately hard.

FEEDING: Use fertilizer in liquid or solid form according to directions.

SPECIAL CARE: Use a mix of fine gravel and clean sand.

PROPAGATION: Seed.

NOTES: *Aponogeton longiplumulosus* is a self-care kind of plant even though it can be a little difficult to keep. This is mostly a problem where there is not enough light and water circulation. Supply a gentle current in the aquarium. Longiplumulosus flowers frequently in open aquaria with adequate lighting, although it is unlikely to produce seeds. The pink to violet—and sometimes white—double flowers are well worth a second look, seeds or no seeds. The plant will die back and observe a rest phase for some period, but then after a few weeks of dormancy, it will send out new leaves, all without help from the gardener. Longiplumulosus is relatively undemanding, and it makes no special demands on water quality.

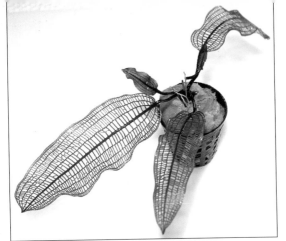

Aponogeton madagascariensis
Madagascar Lace Plant, Laceleaf

OVERVIEW: The Madagascar Lace Plant is among the most sought-after of aquarium plants. Its lattice-like leaves and majestic size make it a true centerpiece. This plant has a reputation for being challenging to keep, however.

HABITAT: Moving waters with dappled sunlight or shade.

NATIVE RANGE: Madagascar and Mauritius.

MAXIMUM HEIGHT: 25 in. (60 cm).

LIGHTING: Moderate, or in shady area of a brightly lit tank.

WATER: 68–72°F (20–22°C); pH: acidic to neutral; hardness: soft.

FEEDING: Requires moderate to heavy feeding.

SPECIAL CARE: _A. madagascariensis_ can be particular about its keeping conditions, requiring medium light, very clean water, and a pH of 7.0 or less. These plants do best when sown in individual small pots where the corm will not be disturbed. Floating plants help subdue the light from above in a brightly lit aquarium. Detritus and algae can become trapped in the open leaf structure and will kill the plant. Place in an area with gentle current that will help keep detritus off the leaves. Plants will probably die back and recover periodically.

PROPAGATION: Seed and crown division. Mature specimens will flower, holding spikes of tiny white flowers just above the waterline. When these flower die off and seeds drop onto fine, rich gravel, new lace plants will grow around the parent plant. This is a slow process, taking from three to four years to produce a full-size plant.

NOTES: Gentle algae eaters such as _Otocinclus vestitus_ (Dwarf Suckermouth Catfish) can help with intricate leaf maintenance.

Aponogeton madagascariensis *is one of the most beloved of the aquarium plants. It's a true aristocrat, but it's almost comical how often it grows to amazing size and vigor for amateurs while confounding the pros.*

Aponogeton rigidifolius
Rigidifolius

OVERVIEW: This slow-growing, unusual *Aponogeton* requires no rest period. It grows on a rhizome much like that of Java Fern (*Microsorium pteropus*) as opposed to the tubers common to the *Aponogeton* genus. The leaves vary in color from reddish brown to olive to bright green, depending on the quality of lighting. New leaves tend to be reddish on the edges with the mature leaves turning brighter green. The leaf margins are gently rippled as well, which makes this a very attractive showpiece worthy of the extra attention required.

HABITAT: Moving waters, both slow and fast with sandy substrate.

NATIVE RANGE: Sri Lanka.

MAXIMUM HEIGHT: 25 in. (60 cm).

LIGHTING: Very bright light.

WATER: 68–82°F (22–28°C); pH: slightly acidic; hardness: soft to moderately hard.

FEEDING: Requires heavy feeding; benefits from supplemental CO_2.

SPECIAL CARE: This is a plant that really needs good water circulation in the aquarium. Place it near the outflow of the filter or in the flow path of a small powerhead. This is not to say that it should be battered by the current, but it does require moving water. Plant the rhizome just below the surface of the substrate.

PROPAGATION: Vegetative propagation through rhizome division. Seed.

NOTES: Use a rich substrate of medium gravel mixed with sand. The flowers are white.

Aponogeton ulvaceus
Ulvaceus, Compact Apono

OVERVIEW: This is an ideal midground specimen plant with light green, translucent, ruffled-edged leaves. The leaves can develop a reddish cast in brighter lighting.

HABITAT: Variable habitats from still to moving waterways in shade and sunlight; found in temporary pools as well as permanent bodies of water.

NATIVE RANGE: Madagascar.

MAXIMUM HEIGHT: 16 in. (40 cm).

LIGHTING: Very bright lighting preferred, but it will thrive in moderate lighting as well.

WATER: 75–82°F (24-27°C); pH: acidic to neutral; hardness: moderately soft to hard.

FEEDING: CO_2 fertilization and nutritious substrate preferred.

SPECIAL CARE: Adequate fertilization, lighting, and space are key to optimal development of this popular *Aponogeton*.

PROPAGATION: Best grown from seed. Rarely by adventitious plantlets.

NOTES: This is one of the most useful of the genus, as it will not become a burden through excessive height and one root can produce many leaves—sometimes as many as 50. There are several varieties; some require dormancy and some do not. Those Ulvaceus with purple flowers are easier to propagate and do not require a rest period, while those with yellow and white flowers are a little more difficult to reproduce and do require dormancy. There are many hybrids of this species, so it is difficult to discern which is the true species.

Aponogeton undulatus
Undulatus

OVERVIEW: Undulatus is an easy-to-keep, hardy species with a wide range of tolerances, making it ideal for beginners. It has long, wide, ruffled, pale green leaves.

HABITAT: Submersed plant grows in still or moving waters.

NATIVE RANGE: Southeast Asia.

MAXIMUM HEIGHT: 16 in. (40 cm).

LIGHTING: Low to bright.

WATER: 72–82°F (22–28°C); pH: acidic to neutral; hardness: moderately soft to hard.

FEEDING: Fertilize regularly. CO_2 not required.

SPECIAL CARE: Though it does well with modest lighting, the leaves will be more intricate and beautiful in brighter light.

PROPAGATION: Young plants grow on stalks that can be separated from the parent and planted in the substrate when they are large enough. Can also be grown by seed.

NOTES: This plant and the many hybrids that are associated with it are often sold in plastic bags in discount stores while in the dormant state. Within a few days of being introduced to the aquarium, they will start to produce leaves.

This splendid plant tolerates a wide range of keeping conditions and keeps growing. Undulatus will serve in the midground or as a specimen. It is not so large that it shadows smaller plants. Some plants seem not to require dormancy, while others die back in the winter months and need to be removed from the aquarium to a cool, moist area. The plant will flower in the aquarium.

Bacopa caroliniana
Giant Bacopa, Blue Water Hyssop

OVERVIEW: Giant Bacopa is an aromatic, easy-to-grow midground to background stemmed plant. Its growth rate is moderate, so there is no concern that this plant is going to take over the aquarium.

HABITAT: This perennial creeping marsh plant grows emersed in shallow areas and submerged in deeper waters. It is sometimes found in slightly brackish waters.

NATIVE RANGE: The southern states of North America and Central America.

MAXIMUM HEIGHT: 24 in. (60 cm).

LIGHTING: Bright.

WATER: 72–77°F (22–25°C); pH: neutral; hardness: moderately soft water preferred.

FEEDING: CO_2 not required. Fertilize regularly.

SPECIAL CARE: No special care required.

PROPAGATION: Easily reproduced from cuttings planted in the substrate.

NOTES: Use a plain gravel or sandy substrate. If allowed to grow emersed, Giant Bacopa will produce attractive blue flowers. Flowers that occur underwater will rot. Plant Giant Bacopa in groups about 2 inches apart for the most attractive effect. The bright, light green, smallish oval leaves will provide a nice contrast to other plants in the aquarium. In very bright light, the leaves may turn reddish. The tender leaves of Giant Bacopa are very tempting to herbivorous fishes, so avoid keeping plant-eating fishes with this plant unless you intend for it to be used as a vegetable fish food.

Bacopa monnieri
Dwarf Bacopa, Baby Tears

OVERVIEW: Dwarf Bacopa is a vigorous plant with short, thick, oval leaves growing on a stiff stem.

HABITAT: Common in fresh and slightly brackish tropical and subtropical waters.

NATIVE RANGE: United States, Africa, Asia, Australia.

MAXIMUM HEIGHT: 16 in. (40 cm).

LIGHTING: Medium to very bright.

WATER: 59–86°F (15–30°C); pH: acidic to alkaline; hardness: soft to hard.

FEEDING: CO_2 not required. Fertilize regularly.

SPECIAL CARE: No special care required aside from adequate lighting and good water quality. Use a fine sand substrate so the plant can anchor well.

PROPAGATION: Cuttings planted in the substrate.

NOTES: Best in bunches, Dwarf Bacopa is a bright green, low-growing perennial herb that is a valuable foreground plant. It does best in high light, so it is often used to carpet the "open swimming area," where only the livestock block light from above. Plant in small bunches. Keep this plant trimmed and tidy. If it starts to "reach" for the light, with the stems becoming longer with more space between the leaves, try to increase the lighting intensity. If the plant becomes leggy, snip the tops and plant them in the substrate. When the water conditions are good, the plant will develop nodal roots. When Dwarf Bacopa grows above the water, it produces small white flowers.

***Bacopa* 'Pantanal'**
Pantanal Bacopa

Bacopa australis
Velvet Hyssop

Bacopa myriophylloides
Brazilian Bacopa

Bacopa sp. 'Red'
Red Bacopa

Barclaya longifolia 'Red'
Orchid Lily

OVERVIEW: The Orchid Lily is an unusual plant indeed. The red form is more common than the green, and both have a reddish hue on the underside of their wavy-margined leaves. The plant grows in a rosette from a large corm that stores nutrients for growth.

HABITAT: Soft, acidic moving waters in areas of both sun and shade.

NATIVE RANGE: Southeastern Asia, New Guinea.

MAXIMUM HEIGHT: 32 in. (81 cm).

LIGHTING: Medium to bright lighting.

WATER: 72–79°F (22–26°C); pH: acidic to neutral; hardness: soft to moderately soft.

FEEDING: Use a nutrient-rich substrate with additional fertilizer in the water column. CO_2 is helpful but not critical.

SPECIAL CARE: Add clay to the gravel substrate. Avoid moving the Orchid Lily, as it tends to suffer from transplant shock, especially if it is moved during the resting period. After recovery from transplanting, however, it grows very well. Potting will delay rampant growth.

PROPAGATION: New plants grow from seeds. If the corm produces more than one plant, it may be divided.

NOTES: New leaf growth is slowed during flowering, so removal of the flower buds maintains the appearance of this showpiece plant. This plant has a relatively large footprint at maturity: be prepared to afford it plenty of room. The green form is not as large as the red form and grows more slowly. The red form requires more light than the green.

Bolbitis heudelotii
African Water Fern

OVERVIEW: The wiry appearance of this unusual amphibious fern belies the delicacy of its nature. It looks like one of the tough guys of the aquatic world, with toothy, dark green leaves borne on a scaly rhizome, but in cultivation it is very particular about the conditions in the aquarium. When kept under its ideal conditions, it grows very well—albeit slowly—and could even be considered hardy once it reaches about 10 inches in size.

HABITAT: This amphibious fern is found both in and beside briskly moving streams and rivers with sandy and rocky bottoms.

NATIVE RANGE: Africa.

MAXIMUM HEIGHT: 20 in. (50 cm).

LIGHTING: Low to moderate lighting.

WATER: 65–77°F (17–25°C); pH: acidic to neutral; hardness: soft to moderately soft.

FEEDING: CO_2 fertilization encourages speedy, vigorous growth.

SPECIAL CARE: Clean, well-aerated water is key to success with the African Water Fern. Other water parameters are also important, but placing the plant in the outflow of the filter or near a powerhead mimics the ecology of its natural habitat.

PROPAGATION: Vegetative, by shoots growing from the rhizome; sometimes by plantlets that develop on the leaf tips.

NOTES: Plant the African Water Fern as you would the Java Fern, by attaching the rhizome to driftwood or porous rocks or other suitable substrate. Suggestions about water chemistry, temperature, current, and light are non-negotiable.

BOLBITIS • LOW LIGHT • CHALLENGING

Cabomba caroliniana
Green Cabomba, Carolina Fanwort

OVERVIEW: Green Cabomba is a fast-growing perennial stem plant that can be a nuisance because of its speedy growth habit. It requires regular pruning or less-than-ideal conditions to keep it from taking over the tank.

HABITAT: Lakes, rivers, streams, and ponds, with slow-flowing and even stagnant waters.

NATIVE RANGE: North and South America.

MAXIMUM HEIGHT: 32+ in. (80 cm).

LIGHTING: Bright.

WATER: 70–76°F (21–24°C); pH: acid to alkaline; hardness: soft to hard.

FEEDING: Micronutrients enhance form and color; CO_2 not required.

SPECIAL CARE: No special care required.

PROPAGATION: Cuttings will root when planted in the substrate. Stem fragments will produce new plants.

NOTES: This is a wonderful background plant for starting new aquariums, where the fast growth is a real asset. Green Cabomba's bright color and delicate-looking, feathery leaves offer excellent contrast for other plants in the aquascape. It is a true aquatic plant that does not grow emersed, though the flowers will poke above the water. Herbivorous fishes are quite fond of Cabomba leaves; goldfish will strip the leaves faster than they can grow back.

The species *aquatica* is also available, in both a red and a green form. It is a mite touchy and demands near-perfect conditions to look worth keeping, however.

Cabomba furcata
Red Cabomba, Forked Fanwort, Cabomba Piauhyensis

OVERVIEW: This stunning stem plant is not the easiest keeper in the aquarium, but those who supply its needs enjoy success. The delicate leaves are fine and fan-shaped, and the color elusive but very highly regarded.

HABITAT: Grows in dense mats in shallow, quiet waters with rich, organic substrates.

NATIVE RANGE: South and Central America and South Florida.

MAXIMUM HEIGHT: 32+ in. (80 cm).

LIGHTING: Very bright light. Natural sunlight is ideal for this species.

WATER: 75-95°F (24-35°C); pH: acidic to moderately acidic; hardness: soft to moderately soft.

FEEDING: CO_2 and macro- and micronutrient supplementation are often required to keep this plant.

SPECIAL CARE: This special-needs species would be delightful in a small, bright, quiet aquarium equipped with CO_2, a fertile substrate, a few invertebrates, and perhaps a pair or trio of small, peaceful fishes. Plant a few stems at a time in layered bunches in areas of greatest light intensity.

PROPAGATION: By stem fragments, lateral shoots, and the seeds of the delightful purple flowers.

NOTES: This plant strives toward the light and will cover the entire aquarium surface. Trim the tops and replant trimmings for freshest appearance. Keep the strongest stems for bushy growth after trimming. Red Cabomba is a great oxygenating plant for the right aquarium.

Cardamine lyrata
Japanese Cress

OVERVIEW: Japanese Cress is a stem plant that has small, light green roundish leaves with slightly jagged edges. Primarily used in the fore- or midground, it provides a nice contrast of color and leaf form. The plant becomes quite bushy if grown under sufficient light.

HABITAT: Marshes.

NATIVE RANGE: Japan, China, Korea.

MAXIMUM HEIGHT: 14 in. (35 cm).

LIGHTING: Bright.

WATER: 59–79°F (15–26°C); pH: neutral; hardness: moderately hard water.

FEEDING: CO_2 fertilization is appreciated.

SPECIAL CARE: Keep this plant trimmed to prevent unsightly straggly stems. It does not tolerate chemicals or pollution well but otherwise is not fussy about water conditions.

PROPAGATION: Cuttings.

NOTES: Without adequate light, this plant will become spindly with weak stems—not attractive at all. Because of its low temperature requirements, Japanese Cress is ideal for use with fishes like White Cloud Mountain Minnows (*Tanichthys albonubes*) and other cool-water fishes. It would seem to be a natural with goldfish, but no such luck—they find the soft leaves quite delectable. Keep the water movement gentle. Japanese Cross will develop nodal roots to extract nutritents from the water. It is also quite happy to grow as a floating plant on the surface of the water close to the light, where it just might produce small white flowers.

Ceratopteris thalictroides
Water Sprite, Indian Water Fern

OVERVIEW: This aquatic fern is extremely versatile. It shows differing forms depending on whether it is rooted in the substrate, floating on the surface, or growing emersed. It's one of those fast-growing, work-horse aquarium plants that is always at your service. Whether it's removing nitrates from the water, harboring tiny fish fry, or served up as a snack for hungry herbivores, Water Sprite is a welcome addition nearly everywhere it is found.

HABITAT: Swamps, marshes, ponds, and river's edges.

NATIVE RANGE: Tropical areas worldwide.

MAXIMUM HEIGHT: 16 in. (40 cm).

LIGHTING: Bright light required.

WATER: 71–82°F (22–28°C); pH: slightly acidic to slightly alkaline; hardness: soft to hard.

SPECIAL CARE: This plant's only real requirement is bright light.

PROPAGATION: Adventitious plantlets.

NOTES: Water Sprite will form a real jungle in your tank if left to its own devices. When it's planted in the substrate, it will form strong, anchoring roots, growing right up to the surface if it can. If it can't reach the surface, the adventitious plants that break free from the parent plant will. Because of this floating habit, the baby plants will need to be harvested frequently so they don't block light to plants below. It will tolerate water movement, but will generally grow better in still areas of the aquarium. The strong roots of the floating plants are excellent hiding places for fry that will feast on the microorganisms that populate the roots.

Cladophora aegagrophila
Marimo, Moss Balls, Tribbles

OVERVIEW: Marimo are velvety soft spheres of algae that have only recently been introduced to the aquarium hobby, though they were described in 1823 from a lake in Austria. By 1920, the Marimo in Japan were protected because of their popularity with tourists (among other reasons). They are ideal aquarium specimens, hardy and unusual, with great color and eye appeal. Marimo outcompete other alga for nutrients, helping to reduce algae in the tank.

HABITAT: Shallow lacustrine waters. They sometimes rise in the water to meet the light.

NATIVE RANGE: Japan, Europe, United States.

MAXIMUM HEIGHT: 12 in. (30 cm).

LIGHTING: Variable, tolerates moderate light as well as high. Maintain a 12-hour cycle.

WATER: 65–82°F (18–28°C); pH: variable; hardness: variable.

FEEDING: Regular fertilization of the water column.

SPECIAL CARE: Avoid allowing a heavy buildup of detritus on the Marimo, which could block light needed for photosynthesis. Squeeze the moss ball into a bucket occasionally to help remove detritus.

PROPAGATION: Division.

NOTES: Marimo are nothing if not versatile. They are super easy to incorporate into the aquarium landscape: just toss them into the tank, and the currents will determine their lodging place. Tufts teased off the main ball can be attached to bark, driftwood, rocks, etc., or attached to netting to fashion a mossy-looking lawn for your aquascape.

Crinum thaianum
Onion Plant

OVERVIEW: This is an interesting-looking plant that doesn't ask much to look good and grow well. The long, ribbonlike leaves sprout from a bulb that resembles an onion, though this plant is not edible. It is a real gem in tanks that have tough fishes, doing especially well with herbivores or rowdy fishes that would destroy more delicate plants. It looks very nice and is unmolested in Malawi cichlid tanks.

HABITAT: Dappled sun-lit streams with moving water and a substrate of sand, gravel, and mud.

NATIVE RANGE: Thailand.

MAXIMUM HEIGHT: 60 in. (150 cm).

LIGHTING: Moderate to bright.

WATER: 72–86°F (22–30°C); pH: acidic to alkaline; hardness: soft to hard.

FEEDING: Use a nutrient-rich substrate.

SPECIAL CARE: This plant grows long leaves that can be trimmed judiciously if they start to look a bit ragged.

PROPAGATION: Sexually and by bulbets that sprout from the main bulb.

NOTES: Use a deep substrate to accommodate the large root struction and to allow the bulb to be planted halfway into the substrate. Keep the water moving and the leaves will soon reach the surface of the water and start to curl around. Use this plant at the back and sides of the tank where it will fill in bare spots quickly. There is a form of Onion Plant found occasionally that has curly leaves.

Crinum aquatica
Natans

Crinum calamistratum
Calamistratum

Cryptocoryne species
Water Trumpets

OVERVIEW: *Cryptocoryne* is an aquarium favorite. The genus carries the romantic common name "Water Trumpet," for the shape of the flower or "inflorescence." Crypts are easily come by in the hobby, and there are many avid crypt fans worldwide who can barely spare a look for any other type of plant. There are about 60 known species at this time, and they each have their quirks.

HABITAT: An assortment of milieu: in rain forests, growing submersed and emersed in bogs and marshes, quiet pools and streams, and flowing rivers.

NATIVE RANGE: Tropical Asia and New Guinea.

MAXIMUM HEIGHT: The smallest, *C. parva,* is just 4 inches tall (10 cm), and *C. aponogetifolia*, said to be the largest, has leaves 18 inches (46 cm) long and 2 inches (5 cm) wide.

LIGHTING: Low to bright, preferably medium.

WATER: 72–82°F (22–28°C); pH: usually weakly acidic to slightly alkaline; hardness: soft to moderately hard. The keeping requirements of the individual species may vary somewhat, as Water Trumpets are found in areas quite different with regard to water chemistry, with some species even found in tidal waters.

FEEDING: These plants do well in a stable environment with rich substrate and small, regular doses of fertilizer. CO_2 supplementation is not required but will help promote healthy growth.

SPECIAL CARE: Crypts are subject to a phenomenon known as "Crypt Melt," where the plant virtually disappears when transplanted. This is a shock reaction to the move, and if the keeping conditions are otherwise acceptable and the rhizome is left in place, the plant will recover and grow all new leaves. The best way to avoid this problem is to avoid sudden environmental changes.

PROPAGATION: By runners and by seed.

NOTES: Crypts should be kept in mature aquaria; they are sensitive to the variable water conditions in new tanks. In aged water, though, these are rosette plants that spread. They are easy to keep once acclimated. The smaller species will fill in an aquarium foreground or midground, thriving in the shade provided by other plants in the aquarium.

With a profusion of species, the genus Cryptocoryne *provides modern aquarium plant hobbyists with a growing array of stocking choices.*

Cryptocoryne albida
Albida
This slow-growing species is not tricky to keep. Give it a nutritious substrate and stable aquarium conditions and it will thrive.

Cryptocoryne balansae
Balansae
Originating from Thailand, this striking specimen plant will do well in hard-water aquaria.

Cryptocoryne beckettii
Beckett's Water Trumpet
Undemanding, and with unique reddish brown leaves, this plant does much to fill in pockets between other species.

Cryptocoryne ciliata
Ciliata
This species prefers harder water and more light than is usual with other crypts.

Cryptocoryne lingua
Lingua

This special little marsh plant with succulent, deep green leaves is best kept in the foreground as a specimen plant and grown partially emersed in a moist, shady environment.

Cryptocoryne lucens
Lucens

This hardy plant thrives in a tank with clean water filtered through mature filtration equipment. Expect about one new leaf per month.

Cryptocoryne parva
Parva

The smallest of the crypts, Parva is perfect for creating a green lawn in the foreground of the aquarium. Place individual plants about an inch apart, and they will fill in quickly.

Cryptocoryne pontederifolia
Pontederifolia, Heart-Leaf Crypt

This is a real specimen plant at 8–10 inches (20–25 cm). Use low light for slow growth or increase light and fertilizer to achieve maximum effect.

Cryptocoryne pygmaea
Pygmaea

This little gem, just 6 inches (15 cm), is from the Philippines and is just coming into the hobby. Give it neutral conditions overall and it will grow slowly but surely.

Cryptocoryne undulata
Undulata

Varies in color from green to dark brown and reaches a height of 4–10 inches (10–25 cm). The ruffled leaves make this a good specimen plant. Good in hard water.

Cryptocoryne undulata 'Red'
Red Undulata

Give this plant neutral conditions and it will steadily produce reddish brown, slightly undulate leaves. The distinctive coloration makes it a good contrast plant.

Cryptocoryne walkeri 'lutea'
Lutea

This useful fore- to midground plant tolerates low light and brackish water. It also prefers cooler temperatures.

Cryptocoryne wendtii 'Broad Leaf'
Wendtii Broad Leaf

This Sri Lanka native is good in hard water and makes a nice filler at 4-8 inches (10-20 cm) in height. It grows slowly, so there's no concern about its taking over the tank.

Cryptocoryne wendtii 'Green'
Wendtii Green

'Green' is one of the favorite crypts. It will grow into a dense carpet in time. It is sensitive to "Crypt Melt," but comes back quickly when it happens. Does well in the shade.

Cryptocoryne wendtii 'Mi Oya'
Wendtii Mi Oya

'Mi Oya' is a gorgeous variety of wendtii with green leaves that are reddish brown on the underside and slightly wavy. It's a native of the Mi Oya River in Sri Lanka and can tolerate warm water.

Cryptocoryne wendtii 'Tropica'
Wendtii Tropica

'Tropica' has hammered, olive-colored leaves and a petite stature. It is undemanding and fills in open areas in the substrate over time.

Cyperus helferi
Helferi

OVERVIEW: This grassy-looking rosette plant is the only one of its genus that is used in the aquarium. It is best used in groups of three or four plants with a bit of water current to enjoy the gentle waving of its slender leaves in a mid- to background planting.

HABITAT: Marshy areas near lakes and streams.

NATIVE RANGE: Southeast Asia.

MAXIMUM HEIGHT: 12 in. (30 cm).

LIGHTING: Bright.

WATER: 75–82°F (24–28°C); pH: mildly acidic to neutral; hardness: moderate.

FEEDING: A rich substrate and the addition of CO_2 will maximize growth.

SPECIAL CARE: Use cooler water until the plant acclimates.

PROPAGATION: By adventitious plants and shoots, as well as rhizome division.

NOTES: This is the perfect aquarium species of the large and diverse genus *Cyperus*, some of which were used by the Egyptians in the making of papyrus. Most of these plants grow emersed and become quite large. *Cyperus helferi* is small enough and tender enough to prosper in the aquarium, and it remains the perfect aquarium citizen, tidy with a slow growth habit. At maturity, the plants send up umbels of flowers that produce tiny adventitious plantlets, replicas of the parent plant, that fall to the substrate where they will root and add density to the planting or that can be planted elsewhere when they have a little size on them.

Didiplis diandra
Stargrass, Water Hedge

OVERVIEW: Stargrass is a soft stem plant with slender stems and needlelike leaves. Somewhat delicate, the fish will have a run at it when it's newly planted. Often, we would fear that it would be a failed experiment in a given aquarium, but then, in just a few days, new leaves would appear and a hardy plant emerge.

HABITAT: The banks of streams and lakes.

NATIVE RANGE: Southern North America, but it is endangered in some states.

MAXIMUM HEIGHT: 16 in. (40 cm).

LIGHTING: Bright

WATER: 75–82°F (24–28°C); pH: slightly acidic to neutral; hardness: medium soft to moderately hard.

FEEDING: CO_2 is recommended along with a nutrient-rich substrate.

SPECIAL CARE: Not a particularly tolerant species, but it's not that difficult either, provided it sees enough light and isn't abused by rough fishes.

PROPAGATION: Stem cuttings; self-propagation.

NOTES: Under bright light with nitrate and supplemental iron, the tips of the leaves will develop an attractive reddish hue. It's most effective planted in small groups. The unique leaf shape and bright green color make it very effective against the shapes and colors of the other plants. *Didiplis diandra* is a compact, delicate plant that is perfect for the middle to front of an aquarium. It will sometimes, when it's extremely happy, suddenly develop pink flowers at the internodes of the stems.

The leaf form in many of the Echinodorus species varies considerably between emersed and submerged aquarium conditions. Many of the larger plants will grow up and out of the aquarium, bearing flowers along the way.

Echinodorus species
Sword Plants

OVERVIEW: The sword plants are one of the most popular groups of aquarium plants. There are more than 45 species described (although this number is a matter of some debate), and exciting new varieties show up regularly to the delight of all concerned.

HABITAT: Sword plants are primarily bog plants in the wild but readily adapt to submersed life in the aquarium, where they will reward attention to their simple needs with healthy growth and reproduction.

NATIVE RANGE: North, Central, and South America.

LIGHTING: Use a timer to keep the lighting on a 12-hour tropical cycle. The leaves grow horizontally where there is less light but will grow vertically and erect when the light is optimal. The amount of light required for individual species is indicated with those species.

FEEDING: Use a deep, nutritious substrate and a fertilizer that contains iron. Sword plants accept a broad range of water chemistries and normal aquarium water temperatures. While the use of CO_2 fertilization isn't strictly necessary, what plant doesn't appreciate the ready availability of carbon dioxide to meet its nutritional requirements? When carbon is in short supply, sword plants will use carbonates from the water, but this is not ideal.

SPECIAL CARE: None noted.

PROPAGATION: Sword plants reproduce readily in the aquarium through root division, adventitious plantlets, and seed. The stalks produce flowers if they reach the surface, but the runners will produce plantlets—daughter plants—as well, especially when submersed. Once these daughter plants have a half dozen leaves, they can be removed from the runner and planted separately.

NOTES: When planting, remove any damaged or yellowed leaves: they will not improve. Also, trim away any damaged or rotted roots. A quick trim of even healthy roots will stimulate them to grow better, so don't hesitate. It is this hardiness that has made the genus famously popular even among those who find it difficult to keep plants in their aquaria. You'll find many types of sword plants called "Amazon Swords," although it was traditionally *E. bleherii* that bore this common name. Now this common name is avoided by those who wish to maintain clarity in identifying sword plants, as the term has been misapplied to many crosses and hybrids. Regardless of the name, a sword plant will be a worthy addition to almost every aquarium.

Echinodorus angustifolius
Angustifolius

OVERVIEW: This pygmy chain sword plant has ribbon-shaped light-green leaves that strongly resemble those of *Echinodorus bolivianus.*

HABITAT: Marshes.

NATIVE RANGE: Brazil.

MAXIMUM HEIGHT: 24 in. (60 cm).

LIGHTING: Medium to bright light.

WATER: 68–82°F (20–28°C); pH: acidic to neutral; hardness: soft to slightly hard.

FEEDING: Use a nutritious sandy substrate and fertilize regularly. CO_2 appreciated but not required. Micronutrients with iron are appreciated.

SPECIAL CARE: None.

PROPAGATION: Runners.

NOTES: This plant resembles *Vallisneria* both in appearance and in habit. It's new to the aquarium scene and doubtless will spread rapidly in the hobby. It likes a sandy substrate where the runners can root easily and take hold before sending out another runner.

Paradoxically, stronger light keeps the plant shorter than medium light. The photo shows a very young specimen; mature plants are quite tall. This is a very easy plant to grow, and soon will need to be thinned and trimmed to keep it from becoming the only species in the aquarium. Because of its height and the way the runners spread out so quickly, it will look best if kept to the sides and back of the aquarium.

***Echinodorus* 'Apart'**
Apart

OVERVIEW: 'Apart' is a hybrid sword plant that was developed from *Echinodorus uruguayensis* and *Echinodorus portoalegrensis*. This is an unusual-looking plant in that the leaves are spread rather flatly across the substrate. Also, there is a somewhat translucent quality to the deeply colored leaves. The newest leaves are reddish brown but become deep green with maturity. All leaves are slightly wavy at the margins.

MAXIMUM HEIGHT: 15 in. (38 cm).

LIGHTING: Medium lighting with some shade and some brightness.

WATER: 72–84°F (22–29°C); pH: slightly acidic to neutral; hardness: soft to slightly hard.

FEEDING: Fertilize the substrate and water; CO_2 not critical but appreciated.

SPECIAL CARE: None.

PROPAGATION: Adventitious plantlets.

NOTES: 'Apart' is a truly unique rosette plant in that one would almost think the plant was not doing well because of the flattened growth habit and the semitransparency of the leaves. This couldn't be further from the truth; this is as it is meant to be. The size, color, and unique appearance make it a highly desirable addition to the planted aquarium. It will not "take over," as so many of the larger *Echinodorus* are wont to do, and the low growth habit puts it front and center in a well-designed layout.

The unusual color, though not readily apparent in this photo, will bring a nice contrast to the fore- or midground of the aquarium.

Echinodorus x barthii
Red Melon Sword

This is a very decorative hybrid that is a perfect specimen plant for aquaria with "neutral" water conditions, i.e., medium in all aspects. The newest leaves are dark red and become dark green at maturity.

Echinodorus cordifolius
Radicans Sword

This sword plant is best suited to a large aquarium. Keep the light to under 12 hours a day to limit growth. Don't be shy about pruning this plant to keep it tidy and of manageable size.

Echinodorus horizontalis
Horizontalis

Horizontalis has much to recommend it in aquarium culture. It doesn't get too big and it is not demanding in any respect. It does grow slowly, though, and is not very fertile. Compared with some plants in this genus, that is an asset.

Echinodorus latifolius
Latifolius

Growing 4-6 inches (10-15 cm) in height, this a fast-spreading grasslike species that will thrive in middle-of-the-road water chemistry and temperature. Use a fine, fertile substrate.

Echinodorus martii
Ruffled Sword, Major

OVERVIEW: The Ruffled Sword is one of the nicest of the sword plants. It's size and fancy ruffled leaves make it a welcome addition in almost every tank. In the larger tanks, it can be used as a specimen plant or in the middleground. In medium-sized tanks, it is fine at the sides and back of the tank. It never sends out nuisance floating leaves, so it is very low maintenance.

HABITAT: Grows both emersed and submersed in marshy areas.

NATIVE RANGE: Brazil.

MAXIMUM HEIGHT: 24 in. (60 cm).

LIGHTING: Medium to bright.

WATER: 75-78°F (17-25°C); pH: mildly acidic to moderately alkaline; hardness: slightly soft to moderately hard.

FEEDING: Use a fertile substrate and occasional addition of micro- and macronutrients. If the leaves turn yellow, add chelated iron.

SPECIAL CARE: Though not necessary, to improve performance, increase light and nutrients; add CO_2.

PROPAGATION: Adventitious plantlets, seed.

NOTES: This beautiful plant tolerates hard, alkaline water conditions in a way that is seldom seen in South American plants. Not only is it lovely, but it is hardy and versatile as well. It does have a fairly dense rootstock, so be sure to give it a good, deep substrate and leave room around the plant for the natural spread of the leaves and roots. Though it will not litter the top of the water with floating leaves, it does have a fairly large footprint within the tank, so plan space for it to spread out horizontally as well as vertically.

Echinodorus 'Oriental'
Oriental Sword

The *Echinodorus* 'Oriental' is a mutation that was discovered in Singapore from *Echinodorus* 'Rose'. This patented plant shows beautiful pink, transparent leaves. Give it a fine, fertile substrate and good light.

Echinodorus osiris
Osiris Sword

Pale leaves are a cry for light and fertilizer from this plant that is known for its red leaves. This is an undemanding plant that offers a nice contrast to the many greens in the aquarium.

Echinodorus 'Ozelot'
Ozelot Sword

This hybrid is very popular in the aquaria hobby. Give it ample light and nutrients and watch the red-spotted leaves darken with age. Remove plantlets to extend the life of the parent plant.

Echinodorus parviflorus
Black Amazon Sword

A compact species that's broader than it is high, Black Amazon Sword grows slowly in low light but more quickly in higher light. The lovely hammered leaves grow in true rosette fashion.

Echinodorus quadricostatus
Chain Sword

Create a foreground lawn or keep the Chain Sword potted for compactness; either way, the light green leaves will make a nice contrast wherever they are planted in the aquarium.

Echinodorus x 'Rose'
Rose Sword

Rose Sword is a strong plant with deep red new leaves that turn almost brown with age. This trouble-free hybrid needs a fertile substrate to ensure good growth. Propagation is by plantlets.

Echinodorus tenellus
Pygmy Chain Sword, Mudbabies

One of the best fore- to midground plants going. Forms a dense clump if given boundaries in the form of rocks or potting. Thrives in a fine sand substrate.

Echinodorus uruguayensis
Uruguay Sword

This gorgeous slow-growing specimen plant improves the aquarium conditions. It thrives in a broad range of temperatures and water chemistries.

Echinodorus tenellus var. 'Tenellus'

The fine leaves of Dwarf Hairgrass lend a very realistic touch to aquascapes that mimic terrestrial scenes.

Eleocharis acicularis
Dwarf Hairgrass, Needle Rush

OVERVIEW: This grassy herb grows flowering stems without true leaves. The flowers, which grow emersed, are tiny, white blossons that show up from June to October.

HABITAT: Moist shoreline areas.

NATIVE RANGE: North America, South America, Europe, Asia, North Africa, Australia.

MAXIMUM HEIGHT: 8 in. (20 cm).

LIGHTING: Bright.

WATER: 64–82°F (18–28°C); pH: neutral to slightly acidic; hardness: moderately soft to moderately hard.

FEEDING: No special requirements.

SPECIAL CARE: Keep the water flow fairly slow, but keep debris out of the "lawn." *Corydoras* catfishes will help keep the rushes clear of waste matter that could smother the plant. Be careful of mosses and algae that are apt to become entangled with the Dwarf Hairgrass and could smother it. Remove any strange plants manually.

PROPAGATION: Runners. Dense plantings can be separated and replanted, which will result in a growth spurt for all the plants.

NOTES: Dwarf Hairgrass is very highly thought of by the admirers of Mr. Takashi Amano's style of aquascaping, where natural scenes are artistically reproduced in the aquarium by different plant species. Contrast in shape and color is celebrated through the use of metaphor. In one design, Dwarf Hairgrass is placed so it looks like rushes at the edge of a pond and the small, dark fishes swimming above simulate a flock of shore birds.

A small group of flowering *Eriocaulon cinereum* with matchhead-like flowers fills in the foreground and provides beautiful contrast in this aquarium. Note the shrimp nestled in the leaves.

Elodea canadensis
Anacharis, Pondweed

OVERVIEW: Anacharis is a fast-growing plant that is not fussy about tropical temperatures. It is perfect for a cold-water aquarium, and indeed is often used with Goldfish, Bettas, and Paradisefish in small, unheated tanks.

HABITAT: Lakes and ponds and sometimes in brackish water.

NATIVE RANGE: North America and introduced into Europe, Australia, and New Zealand.

MAXIMUM HEIGHT: 20 in. (50 cm).

LIGHTING: Moderate to bright.

WATER: 59–68°F (15–20°C); pH: slightly acidic to alkaline; hardness: hard.

FEEDING: No special requirements.

SPECIAL CARE: No special care.

PROPAGATION: Stem cuttings.

NOTES: This plant grows quickly, producing oxygen in the tank. Young plants start from a seedling stem with roots growing in mud; nodal roots occur along the stem, and these are produced at intervals along the stem. This plant can get quite long in the wild—3 meters plus—but in the aquarium, the tops should be cut and replanted for a bushy appearance. Cutting also produces a bushier plant. Anacharis grows rapidly in favorable conditions and can choke shallow ponds, canals, and the margins of some slow-flowing rivers. Other common names include Water Thyme, Common Elodea, and Ditch Moss.

Eriocaulon cinereum
Ashy Pipewort

OVERVIEW: A newcomer to the aquarium scene, this tiny plant is as useful as it is unusual. The rosette shape and strange flower make it welcome in the foreground of high-tech aquaria.

HABITAT: Marshes and bogs.

NATIVE RANGE: Southeast Asia.

MAXIMUM HEIGHT: 3 in. (8 cm).

LIGHTING: Intense.

WATER: 65–77°F (17–25°C); pH: moderately acidic; hardness: moderately soft.

FEEDING: Fine and fertile substrate, macro- and micronutrients, and CO_2 supplementation.

SPECIAL CARE: This high-needs plant is well worth the extra effort required to provide the brightest light and quality nourishment.

PROPAGATION: Division of the rosette. When the plant is ready to divide, the leaves of the rosette will seem crowded and will be growing in different directions. Uproot the plant; on examination, there will be two (or more) distinct plants. Sever the rosettes with a sharp tool and return the new plants to the aquarium.

NOTES: Ashy Pipewort grows slowly but steadily from a large set of roots. Use a fine, deep, fertile substrate to encourage spreading of the roots, which will lead to increased propagation opportunities. When the plant is in good condition and its needs for light, carbon dioxide, and fertilizer are being met, it will send up unusual flower shoots from a yellowish center.

Fissidens fontanus
Fissidens, Phoenix Moss

OVERVIEW: This is a wonderfully easy-to-keep and attractive native American moss that is proving itself very useful in all manner of aquarium applications. It will attach to stone and wood, and even grow as a lawn through craft mesh.

HABITAT: Ponds, lakes, and streams.

NATIVE RANGE: United States.

MAXIMUM HEIGHT: 2 in. (5 cm).

LIGHTING: Low to bright light.

WATER: 65–77°F (17–25°C); pH: accepts a wide range of water conditions; hardness: moderately soft to moderately hard.

FEEDING: Normal tank conditions.

SPECIAL CARE: None.

PROPAGATION: Division; spores.

NOTES: This moss attaches to surfaces in the aquarium with tiny rootlets. It is incredibly diverse in use, with a broad range of conditions acceptable and an ability to grow on virtually any surface. Once established, new fronds will grow from the parent plant every week or two. Eventually, this moss will cover a surface completely. It is used in "topiaries" to create shapes in the aquascape. Once Fissidens is established, it is virtually maintenance free and makes no demands, neither for light, fertilizer, nor encouragement. It is very exciting for the aquatic plant hobby to find such a gem. For years, we had only the same few mosses and ferns that could be used in tough tanks. This adds another very hardy moss to the aquatic gardener's repertoire.

Glossostigma elatinoides
Glosso

OVERVIEW: The low-growing Glosso, one of the tiniest of foreground plants, is often used to carpet the substrate in bright aquaria.

HABITAT: Marshy and boggy areas.

NATIVE RANGE: Australia, New Zealand, and Tasmania.

MAXIMUM HEIGHT: 1 in. (2.5 cm).

LIGHTING: Bright to very bright.

WATER: 72–78°F (22–26°C); pH: mildly acidic; hardness: soft.

FEEDING: CO_2 supplementation increases growth quickly.

SPECIAL CARE: The substrate should be fine and nutritious to increase density of the planting.

PROPAGATION: Lateral shoots.

NOTES: The higher the light, the more compact the growth with this plant. Lower light levels or shady areas will just cause it to melt.

When planting in the aquarium, small bunches of Glosso should be planted deeply at intervals.

Even though this is a tiny plant, Glosso has the ability to form a dense carpet where it is planted, provided its need for light and nutrients are fulfilled. It is often planted in craft mesh to get it started so it doesn't float around the tank. If you see that your Glosso is not performing according to your expectations, look to the lighting and check for overshadowing plants in the midground or background. Also, try to use this plant in a CO_2-supplemented environment.

Hemianthus callitrichoides *is an attractive, useful plant that will cover the substrate completely with tiny leaves, giving the aquarium a wonderfully "finished" look.*

Hemianthus callitrichoides
Baby's Tears

The smallest of the aquarium plants, Baby's Tears is welcomed by aquatic decorators for its delicate appearance. Give it a rich, bright environment and it will thrive. CO_2 supplementation is appreciated.

Hemianthus micranthemoides
Pearl Grass

All this gorgeous little plant needs is strong light and fertilizer and it will take off. In lower light, it tends to grow upward; in bright light, it spreads. Trim it often and plant the trimmings.

HEMIANTHUS • BRIGHT LIGHT • CHALLENGING

HEMIANTHUS • BRIGHT LIGHT • CHALLENGING

115

Hydrocotyle leucocephala
Pennywort

Undemanding, resilient, and bountiful, this floating plant can grow up and cover the water's surface. It excels in breeding tanks, where it provides protection for fry.

Hydrocotyle sibthorpioides
Asian Pennywort

This delicate Asian species is improved by CO_2 and bright light. It starts slowly, but once acclimated, it will grow steadily to its full height of 3 inches (8 cm) and spread over the tank.

Hygrophila polysperma
Indian Swampweed

OVERVIEW: Indian Swampweed is one of the toughest of all the aquatic plants. Depending on where it is growing, the size and shape of the leaves differ.

HABITAT: Marshes and bogs.

NATIVE RANGE: Southeast Asia, and throughout the tropics.

MAXIMUM HEIGHT: 16 in. (40 cm).

LIGHTING: Medium to bright light.

WATER: 71-82°F (22-28°C); pH: slightly acidic to neutral; hardness: soft to moderately hard.

FEEDING: CO_2 is not needed.

SPECIAL CARE: Substrate is optional.

PROPAGATION: Reproduction through lateral shoots; cuttings.

NOTES: Like the canary in the coal mines, if this plant does not do well, aquarium conditions need serious attention, because likely nothing else will grow either—and that includes animals. To increase your stock of this interesting and very attractive plant, just snip the healthy top and stick it into the substrate.

All of the many forms and species of this plant are recommended for aquarium use. (The same cannot be said about their status in the wild, where they are on the Noxious Weed List in many areas.)

Hygrophila spp. grow quickly enough that they can sometimes be used in aquaria with small herbivorous fishes as supplemental vegetable food.

Hygrophila corymbosa 'Stricta', or Giant Hygro, grown emersed.

Hygrophila corymbosa
Hygro

Hygro is a fast-growing stem plant that is happiest in fast-flowing water. Its shoots will be stronger in brighter light. The reddish color intensifies in brighter light.

Hygrophila difformis
Water Wisteria

This plant grows best in a nutritious environment, making it ideal for tropical aquaria, where it will protect fry and help purify the water. Does best in good light.

Hygrophila pantanal 'Wavy'
Hygro Pantanal

This Brazilian plant has moderate growth rate and requires slightly more light than the other hygros. Still, it is an interesting and attractive addition to the aquarium.

Hygrophila polysperma 'Sunset'
Sunset Hygro

No problems with Sunset Hygro, which is quite stunning in good light when the pinks pop. An asset to any aquarium, it's one of the easiest of the stem plants to grow.

Lilaeopsis brasiliensis
Micro Sword, Brazilian Micro Sword

OVERVIEW: A favorite of aquascapers, the bright green color and contained height of this compact grassy plant create a foreground lawn in the aquarium.

HABITAT: Marshes, ponds, banks of slow-flowing rivers.

NATIVE RANGE: Brazil, Argentina, Paraguay.

MAXIMUM HEIGHT: 3 in. (7 cm).

LIGHTING: Will tolerate medium light, but the better the light, the better it will grow.

WATER: 71–78°F (22–26°C); pH: acidic to neutral; hardness: moderately soft to hard.

FEEDING: Nutrient-rich substrate; CO_2 supplementation optional.

SPECIAL CARE: Employ some small *Corydoras* spp. to keep the detritus from smothering the lawn.

PROPAGATION: Runners.

NOTES: Use a fine-grained substrate to hold the delicate roots of this plant. Micro Sword tends to grow in a line, with a little shoot and roots at regular intervals. To plant, group a few of the shoot/root combos and either plant directly into the substrate or gently tie them together with black thread and attach them to a small stone to combat buoyancy. Though they are somewhat slow-growing, they will fill in the entire substrate in time. They even grow in the shade of the taller plants, where they will get a bit taller than those plants that are directly in the light. This plant grows stronger in harder water than many of the tropical plants that have an affinity for soft water.

Limnobium laevigatum
Frogbit
A floating plant that grows virtually anywhere there is light and fertilizer, Frogbit is a great nitrate remover and provides security for fry and shy fishes as it covers the surface of the tank.

Limnophila aromatica
Rice Paddy Herb
High light and CO_2 will have this challenging plant thriving and displaying the reddish coloration and fragrance that makes this herb a treat to keep.

This is the flower stalk of the Cardinal Plant, *Lobelia cardinalis*, when grown in emersed conditions.

Lobelia cardinalis
Lobelia, Cardinal Flower

OVERVIEW: Lobelia is one of the mainstays of the Dutch Aquarium hobby, where the small-leaved plants are used as "streets." The same species produces many shades of color and form, especially when grown out of the water.

HABITAT: Marshes and along the banks of rivers and lakes.

NATIVE RANGE: Central and eastern North America, Canada, and Mexico.

MAXIMUM HEIGHT: 12 in. (30 cm).

LIGHTING: Medium to bright.

WATER: 71-78°F (22-26°C); pH: mildly acidic to mildly alkaline; hardness: soft to hard.

FEEDING: Use a fertile substrate for thicker stems, greener leaves, and an overall "stockier" plant. CO_2 not required.

SPECIAL CARE: Lobelia grows slowly and makes no special demands regarding care.

PROPAGATION: Cuttings and side shoots. Can also be grown from seed.

NOTES: With brighter light, stronger plants develop. Most plants purchased have been grown emersed and will lose their leaves, but the new growth will be smaller and have round leaves as opposed to the larger, pointed emersed form. Plants with small, round light green leaves and purple undersides grow from the withered flowers floating in water. Planted and pruned, they will become the dwarf form that is highly prized in aquascaping. Topping and replanting the shoots will result in bushy growth in the topped plant.

Ludwigia ovalis
Oval Ludwigia

OVERVIEW: This sometimes-touchy, relatively new plant to the aquarium trade is well worth any extra effort required to accommodate it. The unique peachy-pink leaf color works beautifully with the light green shades so abundant in aquatic plants. The entire aquarium will benefit from the extra care it will get because of this plant.

HABITAT: Marshes, lakes, ponds.

NATIVE RANGE: Japan, Taiwan, China.

MAXIMUM HEIGHT: 12 in. (30 cm).

LIGHTING: Medium to very bright.

WATER: 68–78°F (20–26°C); pH: mildly acidic to neutral; hardness: moderately soft to moderately hard.

FEEDING: CO_2 supplementation is not entirely necessary, but the benefits of its use are appreciable. Iron is especially necessary for color. Macronutrients, as well, should be dosed regularly.

SPECIAL CARE: This stem plant is slightly more delicate than other members of the genus *Ludwigia*, but it grows quickly.

PROPAGATION: Side shoots, cuttings, seed.

NOTES: This plant is best suited for a prominent position in the foreground and middle of the aquarium. The main element required for satisfactory growth is sufficient light, which will help maintain color and bushy growth. It's found in cooler waters than are usual in the tropical planted aquarium, but unlike many temperate-water plants, it will do well in tropical temperatures. If the substrate is well fertilized, the roots will be quite thick.

Ludwigia arcuata
Needle Leaf

Needle Leaf grows quickly with lots of light and fertilizer. The red color and unusual leaf shape makes this a plant for contrast and inspiration. It is sometimes confused with *Didiplis diandra.*

Ludwigia inclinata var. *verticillata* 'Cuba'
Ludwigia Cuba

This is a low-growing stemmed swamp plant that is distinguished by the copper-topped leaves it develops in good bright light, with fertilizer and, ideally, CO_2 supplementation.

Ludwigia inclinata 'Green'
Green Inclinata

This plant wants it all. Carbon dioxide, macro- and micronutrients, bright light, and soft water are all on its list of demands, but distinctive and fast growing, it's still worth the keeping.

Ludwigia palustris
Palustris

There are several varieties of this plant; all require the best of conditions to display their special attributes of intense color and the potential of flowering on emersed growth.

Marsilea hirsuta
Water Clover

OVERVIEW: One of the water ferns, this lucky charmer has everything going for it and very little to complain about. It changes form somewhat according to the keeping conditions, but whether it's staying put in low light or virtually skipping along the substrate in the high light, Water Clover is a mighty morpher with a lot of ranges.

HABITAT: Marshes, water.

NATIVE RANGE: Australia, pandemic.

MAXIMUM HEIGHT: 4 in. (10 cm).

LIGHTING: Very low to bright.

WATER: 75–82°F (24–28°C); pH: +/- neutral; hardness: soft to hard tolerated.

FEEDING: Undemanding.

SPECIAL CARE: None required.

PROPAGATION: Runners.

NOTES: The Water Clover is a totally undemanding plant with enormous appeal as a ground cover. Because it is such an easy keeper, it is recommended for hobbyists at every level of experience.

While the four-leaf clover form is whimsical in an aquascape, all of its forms are attractive and form runners that quickly fill in the foreground of the aquarium with a low, dense cover in delicate shades of green. There is not much maintenance required.

Though this plant will do perfectly fine in low light and a variety of water conditions, to see it at its very best, supply it with bright light, nutrients, and a modest amount of supplemental CO_2.

Mayaca fluviatilis
Stream Bogmoss, Silver Foxtail

OVERVIEW: The fine, feathery light green leaves of Stream Bogmoss seem to be just made for waving in a gentle current as it reaches for the water's surface.

HABITAT: In and on the edges of streams, ponds, springs, and lakes, preferably in slightly moving water.

NATIVE RANGE: Southeastern U.S., Central and South America.

MAXIMUM HEIGHT: 24 in. (60 cm).

LIGHTING: Bright to very bright.

WATER: 73–77°F (23–25°C); pH: acidic to slightly alkaline; hardness: very soft to slightly hard.

FEEDING: Nutrient-rich substrate; CO_2 supplementation advised. Add iron if leaves turn pale.

SPECIAL CARE: Give this demanding stemmed plant fine sand to hold the length of it fast in moving water. This common U.S. native species has delicate and soft, fernlike, leaves. Prune with intention, first to encourage bushiness and then to allow height. Keep the stems fresh and producing the lateral shoots that make the plant bushy. Be sure there are no shadowing plants to block available light.

PROPAGATION: Lateral shoots.

NOTES: Place this delicate plant in bunches where it will receive direct light. It's a fast grower and will need to be topped fairly frequently. When allowed to reach the surface, and in adequate light, Stream Bogmoss could produce white or pink flowers that are about 1/2 inch across.

Java Fern is one of the toughest, most useful, best-looking, all-around perfect plants that can be kept in the aquarium. This is Java 'Philippine'.

Microsorum pteropus
Java Fern

OVERVIEW: The Java fern is the star performer in the aquarium: people who cannot grow any other plant can keep it; fish that destroy virtually every other plant cannot destroy it; herbivores do not eat it. All the forms are very attractive and are great aquarium plants.

HABITAT: Emersed along banks of rivers and streams.

NATIVE RANGE: Tropical Asia.

MAXIMUM HEIGHT: 12 in. (30 cm).

LIGHTING: Low to bright light, with medium light preferred.

WATER: 75–82°F (24–28°C); pH: slightly acidic to neutral; hardness: soft to moderately hard.

FEEDING: Java ferns grow slowly and tolerate an environment low in nutrients. The plants derive their nourishment from the water column and not from the substrate, and nutrients are stored in the rhizomes. CO_2 is not required, but will amplify the growth rate.

SPECIAL CARE: Preferred substrates are rocks, driftwood, bark—virtually any rough surface to which the rootlets can attach. Do not bury the rhizome in the substrate; it will rot.

PROPAGATION: The rhizomes can be divided (preferably from the end with new growth). Adventitious plants form on roots and leaves. Browned-off leaves are experiencing sexual reproduction through spores and tiny new plants grow on the dead-looking leaves.

NOTES: In addition to the plants on the following pages, there are varieties called 'Red', 'Undulate', and 'Taiwan', which exhibit differing growth habits.

Microsorum pteropus 'Narrow Leaf'
Narrow-Leaf Java Fern

This cultivar is unusual in that the leaves are quite long and narrow for a Java fern. Like all Java ferns, Narrow-Leaf Java Fern prefers areas with good water circulation.

Microsorum pteropus 'Philippine'
Java Fern

'Philippine' has hammered leaves and grows both emersed and submerged. Tolerates brackish water.

Microsorum pteropus 'Tropica'
Java Fern

Often used in alkaline, hard-water tanks and even brackish-water tanks. Rift Lake cichlids will not harm this Java fern. It is a big plant with toothed leaves.

Microsorum pteropus 'Windeløv"
Lace Java Fern

On the 'Windeløv' variety, the ends of the fronds are divided into fingerlike projections, like a staghorn. This unusual plant readily attaches to irregular surfaces in the aquarium.

Monosolenium tenerum
Pellia

OVERVIEW: Pellia is a liverwort, a living fossil, that has found a fond niche in the aquarium. It has an unusual texture, almost jellylike, with attaching hairlike roots that resemble seaweed. This is a very unique-looking plant, olive green in color, and slightly transparent with a forked leaflike thallus.

HABITAT: A terrestrial plant; grows in moist places where there is high nitrogen.

NATIVE RANGE: India, China, Taiwan, and Japan.

MAXIMUM HEIGHT: 2 in. (5 cm).

LIGHTING: Low to bright.

WATER: 41–82°F (5–28°C), pH: acidic to alkaline; hardness: very soft to very hard.

FEEDING: Though not required, CO_2 supplementation and a well-fertilized environment are optimal.

SPECIAL CARE: None required.

PROPAGATION: Division.

NOTES: Pellia is easy to grow. It is quite rare in the wild, and even threatened in some places, but its success in the aquarium is note-worthy, and it spreads quickly once established. Pellia is known for being brittle and breaks up when handled, which makes it a little difficult to fasten to a substrate, but once it's taken hold, it will form nice puffs wherever it has been placed. The plant uses hairlike fila-ments, called rhizoids, to attach to the substrate.

Myriophyllum aquaticum
Parrot Feather, Water Milfoil

OVERVIEW: The Parrot Feather is a venerable plant of early "goldfish bowl" fishkeeping. It is especially useful in breeding tanks because of the fine, feathery fronds that protect eggs and fry and harbor nourishment for young fishes.

HABITAT: Freshwater lakes, ponds, and canals with slow-moving waters.

NATIVE RANGE: North and South America.

MAXIMUM HEIGHT: 12 in. (30 cm).

LIGHTING: Requires bright light.

WATER: 50–77°F (10–25°C); pH: slightly acid to neutral; hardness: soft to medium-hard.

FEEDING: To see the best of this plant, treat it as you would any valuable species and use CO_2 and a fine, fertile substrate.

SPECIAL CARE: None required.

PROPAGATION: Rhizome division or cuttings. Both male and female plants exist.

NOTES: This plant is a great oxygenator and will do very well in cold-water aquaria. It's one of those plants that you either love or hate. Demanding as far as light is concerned, it will lose lower leaves at the first sign of shade. In an aquascape, Parrot Feather should be topped frequently and the tops replanted. It is at its best when planted in groups, but don't plant the shoots too close together, as doing so will prevent light from reaching the lower leaves. *Do not discard this plant into waterways:* it is a noxious weed where it has been introduced.

Myriophyllum hippuroides
Western Milfoil

The lower stems will quickly lose their leaves if deprived of light. Rhizomes give rise to numerous smaller thinner roots. Emersed stems produce flowers.

Myriophyllum simulans
Red Foxtail

A bunch of Red Foxtail in the brightly lit aquascape is going to turn heads. Take care that algae doesn't smother the delicate leaves, as it can be a problem.

Nesaea pedicellata
Orange African Hygro

OVERVIEW: This unusual-looking species has red stems and green leaves touched with orange. It is sometimes confused with *Ammannia.*

HABITAT: Marshes and pools.

NATIVE RANGE: Tanzania, Mozambique.

MAXIMUM HEIGHT: 20 in. (50 cm).

LIGHTING: Medium to bright.

WATER: 71–82°F (22–28°C); pH: acidic to alkaline; hardness: accepts both hard and soft water.

FEEDING: Does well in normally fertile environment. CO_2 is not required, but it will bring out the best in a plant, namely, the red stems and the orange that occurs on the leaves when in good condition. Dose iron and trace elements at regular intervals.

SPECIAL CARE: None required.

PROPAGATION: Lateral shoots.

NOTES: Subtle in its appearance and good for adding a touch of red to the aquascape, this plant is quite easy to grow and requires little in the way of extra consideration. The growth rate is moderate, which is handy in display tanks, as it doesn't require high maintenance. Good light to the lower leaves is required, however, or they will die off. In bright light, and when allowed to grow emersed, *Nesaea pedicellata* produces small light-purple flowers. Because of its similarity to *Ammannia*, it is sometimes called "Yellow Ammannia."

Nuphar japonica
Spatterdock

A tuberous plant that can get quite large, Spatterdock is ideal in Discus tanks, where the temperatures are generally at the upper range of tropical temperatures.

Nymphaea lotus zenkeri 'Red'
Tiger Lotus

This easy plant is admired for its varied and abundant brightly colored leaves. It will flower with a true night-blooming water lily if given space and nutrients.

Nymphoides aquatica
Banana Lily

OVERVIEW: The Banana Lily is a real aquarium curiosity. The leaves and flowers are nice, and they do resemble the water lily, but it's the roots that draw attention and for which the plant carries the moniker Banana Lily. These roots look remarkably like a bunch of green bananas! The leaves of the Banana Lily are green on top, with purple undersides. The flowers are small, white, and have five petals.

HABITAT: Quiet waters in coastal regions.

NATIVE RANGE: United States.

MAXIMUM HEIGHT: 12 in. (30 cm).

LIGHTING: Bright, likes full sun.

WATER: 68–78°F (20–26°C); pH: slightly acidic to neutral; hardness: moderately soft to hard.

FEEDING: This plant is not a heavy feeder. Nutrients are stored in the thick rootstock.

SPECIAL CARE: Bury the root only halfway into the substrate.

PROPAGATION: Runners or by root division.

NOTES: When the Banana Lily roots, it sends leaves to the surface. The stems develop nodes that produce more leaves, a stem, flowers, and the banana-like roots of a new plant. The original stem will rot, and the new Banana Lily will sink, to take root wherever the environment is hospitable. These plants do not do well in low light, nor in briskly moving water. They are plants of still waters and bright, sunny days.

Pogostemon helferi
Downoi, Little Star

OVERVIEW: This is the newest star in the aquarium world. *Dao noi* in Thai means "Little Star." A perfect foreground plant, Downoi's crinkly edged leaves and starlike shape are unique in the aquarium hobby.

HABITAT: Banks of creeks and rivers, sometimes underwater and sometimes emersed.

NATIVE RANGE: Thailand.

MAXIMUM HEIGHT: 4 in. (10 cm).

LIGHTING: Low to very bright.

WATER: 68–86°F (20–30°C); pH: slightly acidic to neutral; hardness: moderately soft to moderately hard.

FEEDING: CO_2 supplementation is not required for keeping, but it will result in accelerated growth when combined with fertilizers and bright light. Iron supplementation required.

SPECIAL CARE: None required.

PROPAGATION: Runners, seeds.

NOTES: Downoi is not difficult. It reaches for the light and elongates somewhat in low-light conditions, but it continues to thrive all the same. If planted in small clusters, it will soon fill in available space in the substrate, making for very attractive groupings. To increase the population, simply separate the individuals that grow off the main stems and gently plant in the substrate. Where it is grown emersed, Downoi produces small flowers that set seeds, which will in turn result in new plants when set in a fine, fertilized substrate with clean water and good light.

POGOSTEMON • BRIGHT LIGHT • EASY

Pogostemon stellatus
Australian Hygro, Eusteralis

Australian Hygro requires high light, nutrients (especially iron), and preferably CO_2, but if it gets what it needs, the leaves turn a bronze color that is much prized in the aquarium.

Pogostemon yatabeanus
Yatabeanus

Yatabeanus is an Australian plant, very similar to the broad-leaf form of *P. stellatus* (above), but which remains bright green. It grows quickly in a nurturing environment.

Potamogeton gayi
Slender Pondweed

OVERVIEW: This very delicate-looking plant has soft olive green leaves with reddish brown tips. The fine leaves are feathery and work nicely in contrast with other shapes and colors in the aquatic decor.

HABITAT: Ponds, ditches, and quiet lakes.

NATIVE RANGE: Southern South America.

MAXIMUM HEIGHT: 39 in. (100 cm).

LIGHTING: Medium light. Brighter light will result in faster growth, which may not be desirable.

WATER: 60–78°F (16–26°C); pH: moderately alkaline; hardness: moderately soft.

FEEDING: No special requirements. If CO_2 is utilized, micro- and macronutrients must also be supplemented.

SPECIAL CARE: Avoid allowing algae to grow on the fine leaves. This may lead to smothering of the entire plant.

PROPAGATION: Rhizome division.

NOTES: Slender Pondweed is not difficult to keep, but it's slow to catch on at first in the aquarium. After it has settled in, though, the creeping rhizomes may need to be trimmed back, or they will take over. This plant is best contained in groups and placed in the background, as it can reach significant height. Trim the tops to keep the bottoms of the stems from going bare.

This plant is excellent in breeding tanks, where its soft leaves will provide a haven for fry or a depository for eggs.

Ranunculus inundatus
River Buttercup

OVERVIEW: A winsome foreground plant, the River Buttercup is new to the hobby, a perfect new silhouette for the miniature aquascape. The parsley-looking fingers of green will march across the expanse of the substrate, nodding above the tiniest of the substrate covers.

HABITAT: Marshes, and bogs, slow streams, ponds, and lakes.

NATIVE RANGE: Australia.

MAXIMUM HEIGHT: 6 in. (15 cm).

LIGHTING: Bright. Higher light results in shorter stems and more bushiness.

WATER: 75–82°F (20–29°C); pH: slightly acidic to neutral; hardness: slightly soft.

FEEDING: CO_2 injection, along with micro- and macrofertilization and a nutritious substrate, will only improve the condition, appearance, and growth rate of this plant.

SPECIAL CARE: Use a fine, fertile substrate.

PROPAGATION: Runners, rhizome division.

NOTES: The single upright stems with their branched fingerlike leaves look best when planted sparsely so that the distinctive silhouette can be appreciated. Create a whimsical aquascape where the buttercups "tower" over a tiny ground cover like Pearl Grass. Though the River Buttercup is slow starting, it picks up the pace when established, and will need to be thinned to stay healthy. Otherwise, the patch can be kept in place by hardscape borders; rocks can form boundaries for special plants while they draw attention to them in the design.

Riccia fluitans
Riccia, Crystalwort

OVERVIEW: Riccia is a liverwort. What you see is a dense mat of thousands of little individual branched-forked thalli shaped roughly like divining rods. This thalli colony can be manipulated into the shapes and many uses of this amazing plant. The color is a bright cheerful shade of green that absorbs the light and sometimes seems to glow from within.

HABITAT: Nutrient-rich waterways.

NATIVE RANGE: Worldwide.

MAXIMUM HEIGHT: .75 in. (2 cm).

LIGHTING: Medium light preferred. Bright light acceptable.

WATER: 68–80°F (20–27°C); pH: acidic to alkaline; hardness: soft to hard.

FEEDING: Riccia draws nutrients from the water column. It doesn't require CO_2 by any means, but it really takes off when CO_2 is used in the tank.

SPECIAL CARE: Do not let Riccia grow out of control.

PROPAGATION: Vegetatively.

NOTES: It is natural for Riccia to "hook" onto projections and to one another—this is how Riccia builds such impressive colonies. Attach the mass to an object with a fine net to create many shapes in the aquascape. Allow it to tangle with Java Moss for a duplex look. Use it with craft mesh to form a ground cover. Riccia is one of the easiest plants to grow, but watch that it doesn't block light to plants beneath. It's perfect for breeding fish, particularly anabantoids. Riccia will grow emersed.

Rotala macrandra
Red Rotala

OVERVIEW: *Rotala* spp. are "Wish List" plants. These challenging stem plants are highly prized for their intense and varied colors. The wavy leaves are thin and delicate, and without a balance of high-quality nutrients and plenty of light, the plants will simply melt into the substrate.

HABITAT: Quiet, shallow waters and banks, also wet soil.

NATIVE RANGE: Southern India.

MAXIMUM HEIGHT: 24 in. (60 cm).

LIGHTING: Bright, intense light is absolutely required.

WATER: 72–82°F (22–28°C); pH: acidic; hardness: soft to medium-hard.

FEEDING: If CO_2 is not supplied, the "deficit" needs to be compensated with careful attention to the dosage and frequency of the application of macro- and micronutrients. Low nitrite and high potassium result in compact, bushy growth. Use a fertile substrate. Include iron in the fertilization regimen.

SPECIAL CARE: Top and prune the plants to achieve desired shape and size and to maximize light to the entire plant.

PROPAGATION: Stem cuttings.

NOTES: In an effort to preserve CO_2, water circulation is sometimes neglected. Be careful with *Rotala*. It won't tolerate stagnation or poor water conditions of any kind, which makes it a very good indicator plant: high nitrate can cause stunting; pallor indicates a shortage of iron. If all is well, rotalas grow very quickly.

Rotala indica
Indica

Delicate and leafy, Indica grows quickly in good conditions. Not as demanding as the more colorful rotalas, this species brings a nice pinkish color to the aquascape. Cuttings root quickly.

***Rotala macrandra* 'Green'**
Green Rotala

The green form of *R. macrandra* is less demanding than the red form in terms of light and nutrient requirements. It is still a flashy plant, and boasts green and pink leaves and stems.

***Rotala macrandra* 'Variegated'**
Variegated Rotala

This variegated cultivar is as demanding as *R. macandra* in terms of light and nutrient requirements.

***Rotala* sp. 'Colorata'**
Colorata Rotala

An easy keeper, this Asian *Rotala* sp. grows quickly in a low-tech environment. It is rare to find a plant with this much color that will thrive in medium light, so it is very useful.

Rotala sp. 'Green'
Green Rotala

'Green' is easy to grow, demanding no special treatment. It tolerates a wide range of light values, and is more predisposed to creeping across the substrate than *R. rotundifolia*.

Rotala sp. 'Pearl'
Mini Rotala

A tiny plant, great for a nano tank, *R.* sp. 'Pearl', or 'Mini', is best kept in soft, acidic, tropical conditions. Top frequently for bushiness. A challenge, but worth the effort for this dainty gem.

Rotala verticillaris
Wagonwheel
This is the original type-species for the highly prized *Rotala* genus of plants. Grows in soft, acid water and tropical temperatures.

Rotala wallichii
Wallichii
Though it's not delicate, Wallichii does require a bright, fertile environment. Best color is at the tops of the plants, which can be topped and rooted in the substrate.

149

Sagittaria subulata
Dwarf Sag

OVERVIEW: Dwarf Sag is a fast-growing rosette plant, and very popular for its bright green leaves that sport reddish tips in bright light.

HABITAT: Rivers, fresh and brackish.

NATIVE RANGE: Eastern United States and South America.

MAXIMUM HEIGHT: 6 in. (15 cm).

LIGHTING: Moderate.

WATER: 64–82°F (18–28°C); pH: slightly acidic to alkaline; hardness: soft to moderately hard. Brackish water acceptable.

FEEDING: Susceptible to iron deficiency. A nutritious substrate with macro- and micronutrient supplementation is advised for best growth.

SPECIAL CARE: None required.

PROPAGATION: Runners.

NOTES: A useful, attractive foreground plant, Dwarf Sag can be as well kept in the low-tech aquarium as in a fully equipped high-tech setup. It thrives wherever it is planted, requiring neither CO_2 nor very bright light. Periodically, the plant will produce long stems that go to the surface and bear small white flowers. The height usually remains around 3 inches, especially when planted densely, which is where this species really earns its keep. Plants placed 2 inches apart to start will grow quickly, sending runners to all parts of the substrate, forming a dense, grassy plain across the bottom of the aquarium. If Dwarf Sag is not kept densely planted, the plants may sometimes shoot up in height, which is usually to be avoided.

Salvinia natans
Floating Watermoss

OVERVIEW: This charming aquatic fern is a dainty addition to the surface of the open aquarium. The stem is floating, filamentous, and branched. Sets of three leaves form on a stem: two small green hairy ones above water and one that serves as the root structure below the water. These small units reproduce very rapidly, quickly covering the surface.

HABITAT: Standing water: lakes, ponds, pools, ditches.

NATIVE RANGE: Worldwide.

MAXIMUM HEIGHT: 1/2 in. (1.25 cm).

LIGHTING: Bright.

WATER: 68–82°F (20–28°C); pH: slightly acidic to neutral; hardness: slightly soft to slightly hard.

FEEDING: This plant takes its nourishment from the water column, so liquid fertilizer should be used.

SPECIAL CARE: Susceptible to chlorosis if there is insufficient iron.

PROPAGATION: Spores and vegetatively.

NOTES: Floating Watermoss takes light from the plants beneath it, but it also prevents algae by blocking light and using nutrients. This makes it an ideal candidate for breeding tanks and tanks containing nervous fishes, but a very poor plant for high-tech aquaria with other plants that need bright light. Floating plants, as a rule, are best used as the sole species in the aquarium, and with a specific purpose in mind. Otherwise, it is necessary to manually remove as many of the plants as necessary to maintain enough light to the lower reaches of the aquarium.

Shinnersia rivularis
Mexican Oak Leaf

OVERVIEW: Mexican Oak Leaf is aptly named, as the leaves are oak-leaf shaped, a unique feature among aquatic plants. It is great for filling in bare spaces quickly, as it grows at an amazing rate without carbon dioxide. The surface leaves, which will try to grow emersed, will get reddish under the right light. This plant needs regular trimming to keep it looking nice in the aquarium.

HABITAT: Streams and rivers with slow-moving waters. Plants rooted in muck.

NATIVE RANGE: Northern Mexico, Texas.

MAXIMUM HEIGHT: 39 in. (100 cm).

LIGHTING: Bright.

WATER: 64–86°F (18–30°C); pH: alkaline; hardness: hard.

FEEDING: Use micro- and macronutrients in the water column. CO_2 supplementation is not required.

SPECIAL CARE: Regular pruning necessary to keep the plant in check.

PROPAGATION: Cuttings, rhizome division.

NOTES: In the aquarium, *Shinnersia rivularis* probably grows faster than any other aquatic plant. The distance between leaves increases in insufficent light. Top the plant, and replant the shoots when the bottom leaves start to look straggly. This plant is not recommended for use in aquascaped tanks unless they happen to be very large and are using large plants. It is ideal for tanks that need hungry plants to help keep the water quality up to par.

Tonina sp. 'Belem'
Belem

This Brazilian stem plant grows to 8 inches (20 cm) in an acidic, soft-water, tropical blackwater environment. It is quite demanding and requires a high-tech setup.

Tonina fluviatilis
Fluviatilis

This delicate stem plant requires the same treatment as *Tonina* sp. 'Belem' (above). Top-prune 2 inches of stem to prevent legginess.

Vallisneria spiralis
Jungle Val

OVERVIEW: The long, strappy leaves of the the *Vallisneria* spp. are among the most familiar of the aquatic plants. Easy to grow and undemanding in all regards, this plant is perfect for beginners and experienced aquarists alike.

HABITAT: Still or flowing waters, usually forming a dense monoculture. Estuaries, lakes, water courses, and wetlands.

NATIVE RANGE: Cosmopolitan.

MAXIMUM HEIGHT: 22 in. (55 cm).

LIGHTING: Medium.

WATER: 59–86°F (15–30°C); pH: alkaline; hardness: moderately hard to hard. Brackish water is acceptable.

FEEDING: Use a nutritious substrate and normal applications of fertilizer in the water. Periodic applications of iron are appreciated. CO_2 supplementation is not required.

SPECIAL CARE: Do not bury the crown. Place the roots gently in the substrate, but keep the juncture of roots and crown above the gravel.

PROPAGATION: By runners, seeds develop from flowers.

NOTES: One of the easiest plants to grow, vals are often the only plants in the aquarium. They are especially admired when planted densely around the back and sides of the aquarium with the tops floating on the substrate. Angelfish look particularly well in this environment. Because Jumgle Val can spread fairly quickly, it may need to be potted in some aquaria to contain rampant growth.

Vesicularia species
Java Mosses

OVERVIEW: Aquatic mosses are exceptionally useful and well regarded in the aquarium hobby. The "Java" mosses include the familiar Java Moss (*Taxiphyllum barbieri*) and newer forms that are showing up: Christmas Tree Moss, Singapore Moss, Weeping Moss, Erect Moss, Creeping Moss, and others.

HABITAT: Clinging to rocks, tree trunks, and virtually any other holufast in water and emersed in moist areas.

NATIVE RANGE: Southeast Asia, Amazonia.

HEIGHT: 6 in. (17 cm).

LIGHTING: Low to bright light.

WATER: 59–86°F (15–30°C); pH: variable; hardness: variable.

PROPAGATION: Spores; division.

NOTES: True wonderments, mosses will grow floating free or attached to an object (rock, wood, ornament, plastic needlepoint mesh, etc.). The root filaments of the moss anchor themselves to these objects, then grow slowly but steadily. A variety of materials is used to anchor the mosses, everything from fishing line to ladies' fine hairnets. Trim as desired, and use the clippings to make new arrangements or to remove them from the aquarium.

These mosses are ideal for breeding fishes. The fry find sanctuary and food in mosses, and often the first sign of new life in the aquarium is tiny flashes of silver in the "Mommy Moss."

Acorus variegatus, *Sweet Flag*, or *Japanese Rush*, is used along pond margins and at the edges of water gardens, not in the aquarium.

The big, the bad, and
the unlikely to survive

There are so many aquatic plants to fill the most beautiful aquariums that I am always mystified when I see people selling and buying plants that are inappropriate for aquarium use. One possible reason could be that the terrestrial species sold do last for some weeks in the aquarium, and the people who use them are terrified of losing the true aquatic plants that we so admire. It's true that when aquarium plants are mishandled some of them can die off very quickly, and after a few bad experiences, it is conceivable that the brown-thumbed aquarist would be tempted by a tough-looking *Dracaena* or *Acorus*. Yes, they will last for some weeks, but in the end, the hobbyist would have fared better with plastic plants, because not only do these plants die off in the tank, but they make little or no contribution to the water quality for the duration and eventually rot in the water, possibly creating a toxic environment.

Though the leaf and pattern are very beautiful, Dieffenbachia *is a terrible choice for the aquarium. Not only will it rot, but the plant is poisonous, and one wonders if the fishes are in some way affected by "Dumb Cane."*

When planting an aquarium, it is far better to provide the conditions necessary to grow aquarium plants than to try to "fake it" with terrestrials. There are aquatic plant species that will thrive in virtually every type of aquarium. With just a little know-how, even the beginning aquarist can have a beautiful planted aquarium. The fact that some fishes will eat, unplant, or make confetti out of tender aquatic plants should not keep one from enjoying the bright greenery that makes an aquarium come to life. There are toughies in the aquatic plant world along with the delicate flowers, and even the most relentless plant-hating cichlid will not chow down on Java Moss, shred the Java Fern, nor dig up a well-planted Onion Plant.

Some of the plants that are guaranteed not to thrive underwater are simply terrestrial species, but some are indeed marsh or bog plants that require high light and humidity but cannot tolerate full submersion permanently.

Caladium bulbs could by some stretch of the imagination be associated with the aquarium because of the few small leaves that appear before they melt away (leaving a nice bit of a mess in their wake). Keep these garden beauties for a shady spot at pond's edge or under a hedge, not your aquarium where they could take a few fish with them as they rot away.

It may be beautiful, but leave Caladium *in the garden, or even pondside, not in your aquarium.*

Non-Aquatic Plant Species

Aluminum Plant (*Pilea cadierei*)
Arrowhead (*Syngonium podophyllum*)
Bamboo Plant (*Bamboo sp.*)
Chameleon Plant (*Houttuynia cordata*)
Chinese Evergreen (*Aglaonema simplex*)
Club Moss (*Lycopodium sp.*)
Coconut Plant (*Calamus sp.*)
Dwarf Rush (*Acorus pusillus*)
Dragon Tongue (*Hemigraphis repanda*)
Dwarf Onion Plant (*Zephyranthes candida*)
Dumb Cane (*Dieffenbachia sp.*)
Elephant Ear (*Caladium sp.*)
Green Sandy (*Dracaena borquensis*)
Hedge (*Alternanthera sp.*)
Japanese Rush (*Acorus sp.*)
Mondo Grass (*Ophiopogon japonica*)
Peace Lily (*Spathiphyllum tasson*)
Pineapple Plant (*Dracaena compacta*)
Pongol Sword (*Chlorophytum bichetii*)
Pothos (*Philodendron sp.*)
Prayer Plant (*Maranta leucoreura*)
Princess Pine (*Lycopodium obscurum*)
Purple Waffle (*Hemigraphis exotica*)
Red Dracaena (*Cordyline sp.*)
Rush (*Pontederia cordata*)
Sandy (*Dracaena sanderiana*)
Scarlet Hygro (*Alternanthera sessilis*)
Silver Queen (*Aglaonema sp.*)
Spider Plant (*Chlorophytum bichetii*)
Stardust Ivy (*Syngonium sp.*)
Sweet Flag (*Acorus calamus*)
Ti Plant (*Cordyline terminalis*)
Underwater Palm (*Chamaedorea elegans*)

Note: This list is by no means exclusive. If it *looks* like a houseplant, it probably is one.

Acorus pusillus
Dwarf Rush

An Asian marsh plant that is ideally suited to the garden pond, Dwarf Rush is so slow growing in the aquarium that it always seems to be on the brink of dying off.

Alternanthera ficoidea
Cherry Stem Hedge

The Cherry Stem Hedge, or Joseph's Coat, is a bedding annual. Keep it in the garden and water it well.

Chamaedorea elegans
Underwater Palm
This plant may look attractive in the aquarium, but don't be fooled. It's not happy when completely submerged in water.

Dracaena borquensis
Green Sandy
When planted in soil, this plant can get taller than a grown man. It's a tough terrestrial species.

Dracaena compacta
Pineapple Plant

Ideal for terraria and paludaria, but the Pineapple Plant is sad in the aquarium. It is a terrestrial plant that is an ideal houseplant.

Hemigraphis exotica
Purple Waffle

Grows best in an east or west window or in partial sun to partial shade. Keep the plant's roots moist, but out of the aquarium!

Spathiphyllum tasson
Peace Lily

The Peace Lily is not for underwater culture. It is, however, very good in boggy areas, such as beside the pond.

Zephyranthes candida
Dwarf Onion Plant

Stick with the *Crinum* spp. for aquarium use. Leave these onions in the lawn.

Herbivores and excavators

The following list names some of the species unsuitable for the planted aquarium. Some are too boisterous, some will eat your plants, and some will just dig all day. When choosing tenants for your planted aquarium, avoid these animals:

Catfishes Large catfishes are out of the question in most planted tanks. A full-sized pleco is an oaf that will swim roughshod through the planted tank at night, never mind that it is so quiet by day. Other catfishes, like the Red-tailed Catfish, are simply too big.

Characins Large characins, like pacus and piranhas, are not welcome in the planted tank. They are highly destructive. Likewise, large barbs, such as the Tinfoil and T-Barb, will wreak havoc in the planted aquarium.

Cichlids Many of the larger cichlids like Oscars, *Geophagus*, and most African cichlids are unsuitable for planted tanks either because they will dig up the plants or they will shred them just because. Most territorial fishes will cause trouble in the planted tank sooner or later.

Cyprinids The Chinese Algae Eater, *Gyrinocheilus aymonieri*, may eat algae when young, but it's both aggressive and useless as an algae eater when it gets larger. Don't put this fish in your planted tank. You will only have to tear up the tank later to remove it. Goldfish are not good candidates for the planted tank, as they will consume any soft plant they can get at.

TOUGH PLANTS FOR ROUGH TANKS

- *Anubias* spp.
- *Crinum* spp.
- *Microsorum pteropus*
- *Vesicularia* spp.

These plants are generally safe with any fish, as they are rugged and some simply taste bad. Floating plants are usually fine with all fishes as well.

Perfect peaceful pets

One important thing to keep in mind when adding fishes and other animals in the planted aquarium is to stock very lightly. If you aren't keeping many animals, make them your best favorites! The following species, though certainly not inclusive, can be recommended for planted aquaria:

Anabantoids Bettas and gouramis are good citizens for the planted aquarium, they may nibble a little, but no harm done. Bettas will drape themselves over the leaves of the plants like a chanteuse on a baby grand, and from there survey the kingdom.

Catfishes Most small catfishes are good and helpful neighbors in the aquarium. *Corydoras, Brochis, Aspidoras, Ancistrus, Otocinclus,* and *Farlowela* are but a few of the best catfishes. The Gold Nugget (*Baryancistrus* spp.) and the Zebra Pleco (*Hypancistrus zebra*) are trophy fish that also will not molest plants.

Characins These include the very best small schooling fishes to adorn the aquarium. The small tetras, headstanders, pencilfishes, and hatchetfishes are but a few of these excellent choices.

Cichlids Angelfish, discus, and dwarf cichlids are all very suitable. They will all utilize the planted aquarium in their spawning activities, but do not damage the plants at all.

Cyprinids The most famous and useful of this clan, the Siamese Algae Eater, *Crossocheilus siamensis,* and the Flying Fox, *Epalzeorhynchus kalopterus,* are good community member and hungry for algae. Rasboras, danios, and some of the smaller, peaceful barbs are also good choices.

Livebearers All livebearers, guppies, mollies, swordtails, platies, etc., are suitable for planted tanks.

Loaches, Killifishes, and Rainbowfishes All are ideal planted tank inhabitants, except possibly for larger loaches.

Other than fishes, many planted tanks are home to a selection of snails, shrimps, lobsters, crabs, and frogs. Contrary to common belief, most snails will not damage plants, and the Malaysian Trumpet Snail (*Melanoides tuberculata*) is very helpful in aerating the substrate. Small shrimps, like *Neocardinia* spp., consume algae.

A small, but efficient CO$_2$ diffuser disperses tiny CO$_2$ bubbles into the aquarium water, providing a ready source of carbon for amazing plant growth.

Feeding and fertilizers

Photosynthesis provides the energy for much of an aquatic plant's growth, but nourishment in the form of fertilizer and trace elements is needed as well. There is an almost magical state in some aquariums in which there is just the right amount of light, number of fishes, water changes, types of plants, and where no extra fertilizer or other amendments are made. The whole aquarium glows with well-being that is natural and seemingly "just happened." While there may have been few deliberate attempts to enhance the system, it works, and obviously works well. Some tanks and their owners are lucky like this, but difficult to duplicate, sometimes taking years to achieve this state of perfection. In other instances and with "green thumb" aquarists, it happens with the very first planted tank, especially when the tank is fully planted at the outset, bacterial cultures are used, and there are few animals in the aquarium.

Some successful aquatic gardeners do not add fertilizer of any kind, relying on fish wastes and small water changes to provide nutrients for the plants. This is not the "scientific approach" preferred by avid enthusiasts.

Fertilizer designed for aquarium use is usually essential if you want to grow beautiful, healthy aquatic plants. Fish wastes, especially in a relatively new aquarium, just will not do the job. Yes, the fish will provide a certain amount of natural fertilizer, but it takes up to a year for a lightly stocked aquarium to be "fertile" enough to support a decent planting, if it ever becomes fertile enough at all. What's more, this fish fertilizer, while it is beneficial to plants, is not complete. Fish waste, both leftover food and food that has passed through animals, provides some nitrate and phosphate, both of which can create massive problems from algae; other missing elements must be supplied by the aquarist in the form of commercially prepared fertilizer designed for aquarium use.

There are degrees of success in the planted aquarium, however, and there is a vast improvement in the growth rate and vigor of the plants in a high-tech aquarium where every detail of the operation—fertilization with CO_2 gas, micro- and macronutrient supplementation, enriched substrate materials, and lighting—is deliberately manipulated for high performance. It is only through water testing, precision techniques, and consistent attention to detail that the breathtakingly lush masterpieces we see with the "Dutch Aquarium" and Amano's "Nature Aquarium" schools are possible (see page 178).

There are several methods of adding nutrients to the aquarium for optimal plant growth: nutrient-enriched substrates, liquid fertilizers (and liquids made from dry powders), and solid tablet fertilizers. The use of nutrient-rich substrate material is gaining broad acceptance, as a fertile substrate is achieved without the long process of accumulating mulm (organic detritus—the underwater equivalent of compost) and messing about with adding garden soil and other organic materials to the inert substrate when setting up a new tank. These nutrient substrates deliver the nutrients to the plant roots in a form that the plants can use very efficiently. Sometimes nutrient substrates are used buried layers under other substrate materials. The nutrient substrates will lose potency after two or three years, but by then the aquarium will have an accretion of organic waste that will provide nutrients indefinitely.

Whatever the substrate, most successful aquarists feed their plants. The previously mentioned caveat about "designed for aquarium use" is important. Fertilizers formulated for regular house and garden plants are not guaranteed to be safe for aquatic organisms. There are countless brand-name aquarium plant fertilizers in the hobby, and it is advisable to use them according to instructions and observe the results. In high-tech aquaria, light, carbon dioxide injection, and fertilizer dosing is a highly choreographed combination of

This bright, cheerful aquarium has plenty of open swimming room for the fishes.

This dwarf Riccia *is producing copious oxygen bubbles as a byproduct of photosynthesis. The oxygen bubbles could cause this mat of* Riccia *to float around the tank if it is not well anchored.*

art and science that results in intensive botanical aquaculture.

Liquid fertilizers that contain macro- and micronutrients must be used according to the manufacturer's directions, as dosage and frequency are important. Overdosing can cause algal outbreaks. Underdosing is less of a problem. Liquid fertilizers are added every week or every two weeks.

Tablet fertilizers provide targeted fertilization to specific plants that may require additional fertilizer. Some plants, like *Echinodorus*, for example, are very hungry for iron, which is available in the usable chelated form to the roots with tablet fertilizers. Place the tablets into the gravel bed to deliver the nutrients right to the plant's roots. If the plant growth is thick and the tank deep, you may wish to use long-handled tweezers or tongs to place the tablets. Each tablet slowly releases nutrients and usually lasts up to one month.

MACRO- AND MICRONUTRIENTS

Plants need the macronutrients nitrogen (N), which they derive from nitrogenous compounds in various forms, phosphorus (P), and potassium (K). Micronutrients, the other elements essential for healthy plant growth, are only needed in trace amounts. Iron, boron, and manganese are a few of the necessary micronutrients. Without them, plants will exhibit a variety of deficiency symptoms, such as yellowing leaves and retarded growth. It is far better to use a good all-purpose fertilizer with trace elements and to change your water regularly, gently siphoning off the gross detritus from the substrate, than to overfeed the aquarium and conserve excess mulm in the hope that it will be the ultimate plant-growing medium. Gross waste products should not be left in the system to be "used" by the plants. In high-maintenance tanks, the accumulating debris from fish wastes and plant leaves should be removed from the aquarium by siphon or gravel vacuum, or allowed to find its way into the filter, where it can be screened out or broken down by nitrifying bacteria into a more usable form.

One tip taken from serious hobbyists is the practice of feeding live foods to the fishes in an effort to ensure that there is no leftover food flakes or pellets in the tank to upset the balance of nutrients.

NITROGEN

Nitrogen (N) is the first of three major nutrients that are essential to plant survival. Combined with phosphorus (P) and potassium (K), these three "macronutrients" are needed in large quantities for plants to flourish. Just as humans need oxygen, protein, and carbohydrates to function properly, plants have the same reliance upon the macronutrient group. Plants require nitrogen to construct biopolymers and proteins. Nitrogen is also an important component of chlorophyll, and it is critical to a plant's ability to absorb and convert light energy.

PHOSPHORUS

Phosphorus (P) is the second of three major nutrients that are essential to plant survival. Phosphorus, along with nitrogen, is an essential element in the formation of chlorophyll in plants. Phosphorus also aids in the formation of necessary energy components such as sugars and starches.

POTASSIUM

Potassium (K) is the third major nutrient that is essential to plant survival. Along with nitrogen, plants require large amounts of potassium to grow well. Also a major component of photosynthesis, potassium is crucial in a plant's ability to absorb and convert light energy into growth.

MICRONUTRIENTS

Micronutrients, as opposed to the three macronutrients (NPK), are elements that are essential to healthy plant growth but are only needed in trace amounts. Iron, boron, and manganese are only a few of the micronutrients that are necessary for plant growth, and without them plants will exhibit a variety of deficiency symptoms. A proprietary blend of micronutrients, pfertz™ micros, is designed specifically for the needs of planted aquariums.

CARBON DIOXIDE

Carbon dioxide (CO_2) and water are used by the chlorophyll in plants to manufacture food (glucose) through the action of light (photosynthesis). It is the nature of carbon dioxide to slowly escape from the

Ancistrus dolichopterus, *the Bristle-nosed Catfish, is a willing worker on algae patrol that does not generally damage desirable species in the aquarium.*

This lacy-leaved Java Fern, Microsorum pteropus *'Windelov', is an aquarium asset, growing in moderate light and having no special care requirements.*

water and join the rest of the CO_2 gas in the atmosphere, and this tendency is facilitated when we aerate our aquariums to provide more oxygen for the fish.

This can leave the plants in short supply of carbon dioxide. When free CO_2 gas is not available for the plants in the aquarium, they will fill their CO_2 needs from carbon molecules present in other forms in the water, which in turn will cause the pH of the water to rise. So while a reduction in the pH of the water could be the result of a buildup of fish wastes or a dirty filter, a rise in the pH is probably indicative of low CO_2 levels. If your pH has increased (and you haven't added any chemical designed to raise the pH), it is a good indication that additional CO_2 would benefit your aquatic plants.

In the lightly planted aquarium, adjustments can be made that will increase CO_2 available to your plants. You can add more fish and reduce aeration. In a heavily planted show tank, there is strong competition for CO_2, and you might want to look into additional CO_2 fertilization.

The addition of CO_2 to the water is a relatively simple process involving a CO_2 generator or a canister of CO_2 gas and a diffuser to control the release of gas into the aquarium. Before beginning any CO_2 fertilization, you must check your carbonate hardness and pH (see pages 26 to 29). If the carbonate hardness is between 65 and

110 ppm, CO_2 fertilization is appropriate. Below this level, the hardness must be increased before adding CO_2 to ensure that the pH will not plummet. If the pH is low, below neutral, the cause must be found before attempting CO_2 fertilization. A series of water changes and good tank maintenance should correct this problem.

CO_2 can be supplied by means simple or sophisticated. The simplest CO_2 delivery system involves plant and fish respiration and the breakdown of waste products by bacteria in the aquarium (and filter). This is not adequate for more than sustaining life in a planted aquarium with an appropriately low fish load. Carbon dioxide powders and tablets that are simply tossed into the aquarium at intervals suggested by the manufacturer can be used to increase CO_2 levels in the water on a small scale. A little farther up the ladder are the simple CO_2 "bells," which are with filled chemicals that react to produce CO_2 that is released into the water over about a month's time.

Do-it-yourselfers will find helpful and inexpensive kits to which yeast and sugar are mixed in a closed canister with the gas vented off through airline tubing and diffused into the aquarium. In the

It's easy to attach Java Fern to a bit of driftwood with cotton thread. When Java Fern shows brown leaves, don't toss them. They brown off just before producing new leaves.

simplest form, a 2-liter soda bottle is cleaned, equipped with a cap that has nipple-type bulkhead fitting, and connected to a length of silicone tubing and some sort of diffuser in the aquarium.

A fermentation is created by mixing water (2 cups), cane sugar/sucrose (2 cups), and 1/4 teaspoon of baker's, brewer's, or champagne yeast. Such a mixture will generate CO_2 for two to three weeks and produce enough carbon dioxide for a 30-gallon planted aquarium. (An excellent article by John LeVasseur on building and operating a do-it-yourself CO_2 system can be found on the Internet by searching for "DIY CO_2 System.")

Various inexpensive commercial kits are also available for basic CO_2 generation. Be sure to use a good diffuser, as this is the crucial link in any system.

For the freshwater equivalent of the reefkeeper in the marine aquarium hobby, there are many types of sophisticated carbon dioxide injector systems that use "paintball-style" cartridges or a full welder-size pressurized canister to deliver CO_2 to the aquarium. These systems operate with controllers or timers and the CO_2 system is either turned off at night or an airstone is turned on to aerate the aquarium and prevent a dangerous pH crash. (At night, plants do not use CO_2, so it must either be stopped or off-gassed.)

Carbon dioxide fertilization works. Plants grown in carbon dioxide-supplemented waters are outstanding. There is a goodly segment of the aquarium plant hobby that relies heavily on carbon dioxide supplementation to achieve their dream tanks. For these hobbyists, CO_2 is a necessary luxury.

When using CO_2 injection, the light levels and amount of fertilizer required are somewhat increased and need to be adjusted accordingly.

Routine maintenance

In fish-only tanks, gravel hygiene is extremely important. The gravel is often swirled and deeply vacuumed to prevent it from compacting and allowing pockets of poisonous gases to develop. However, for planted tanks, you want to disturb the roots as little as possible. Light vacuuming of the surface layer is permissable if you use a large-mouth vacuum tube and smaller hose to avoid sucking out

The Angelfish would use any vertical plant leaves to lay their eggs. These vertical-substrate spawners are well known to favor sword plants as spawning sites.

the gravel. A layer of coarser gravel over the finer substrate permits surface cleaning, but you should not plunge the vacuum tube into the gravel. Very lightly siphon up floating debris when doing water changes; rotting material can use up too much oxygen and provide a home for unwanted bacteria.

PRUNING WITH PURPOSE

Pruning a gardening art and no less so when keeping aquatic plants. It should be performed thoughtfully with an eye toward improving the health and appearance of the plant. Plants grow and parts of plants die; pruning is necessary in both cases. When plant leaves start looking a bit shaggy, get rid of them. The dying or damaged leaves are taking strength from the entire plant. Decaying leaves join fish waste and leftover food in creating water-quality problems. Don't hesitate to remove them from the aquarium.

Pruning can also stimulate your plants. Cutting back floating leaves that have outgrown the main plant (often the case with Banana Plants) will keep the plant young longer and keep the growth energy concentrated in the main plant.

If the plants are permitted to become overgrown, the parts of the plant that aren't getting enough light will become bare-stemmed, a condition characterized by heavy growth at the waterline while the view near the gravel reveals a fine collection of bare stems. Keep top-trimming your stemmed plants so they stay bushy rather than leggy.

Pruning encourages new growth. When the new buds are removed from plants like *Cardamine* and *Hygrophila*, the plant puts its energy into the formation of new roots, giving you a compact, bushy plant. Fine-leafed plants like *Myriophyllum* and *Cabomba* will grow side shoots when new growth is pruned. Water Wisteria also becomes much fuller when new buds are removed. Some plants, such as *Sagittaria* and *Acorus,* show their best leaves in the new growth, which is more attractive than the older leaves. In these cases, if pruning is necessary or desirable, take the old growth and leave the brighter, younger leaves.

ALGAE CONCERNS

Some forms of algae can be attractive and good for grazing fishes, but algae growth in the planted aquarium is usually best avoided. You can use natural algae controls in the form of algae-eating fishes like *Otocinclus* or Siamese Algae Eaters, but a better strategy is to avoid the conditions conducive to an algae takeover.

Algae thrive in situations where there are excessive organics

Crossocheilus siamensis (Siamese Algae Eaters) are very helpful in keeping the tank clear of nuisance algae.

This restrained use of just a few species of low-light plants, combined with a school of just one species of tetra, makes this a very tasteful display of aquatic harmony. Even though the fish and plants are from different localities, they share the same requirements in the tank and work well together.

(fertilizers) in the water and in high light. Under normal circumstances, algae should not be a problem in the planted aquarium, as the higher life forms (aquatic plants) out-compete algae for nourishment. If you do notice an algae bloom starting up, combat its growth by holding off on the fertilizer, scrape the algae off any surface you can, increase the volume and frequency of your water changes, and add more aquatic plants.

Overfeeding of fishes can easily contribute to algae blooms and persistent growth of nuisance algae. Be sure all food is eaten up within minutes of each feeding session and that leftovers are not allowed to settle into the plants or substrate. The masters of underwater gardening use great care not to overstock their tanks. Many feed only live foods or floating flakes to avoid having uneaten rations become trapped in the system to decay and lower water quality.

In a fish-only tank, algae can be controlled by reducing the intensity or duration of lighting each day or even going for a period without light, but this is risky in a planted tank.

33-GALLON TANK. *The Dutch-Style of aquascaping has a long history and focuses on tidy plots of colorful plants that point to a central focal point with the lower plants in front and taller ones at the sides and back, giving the impression of a well-tended garden with paths, or avenues, of plants. There is generally not much hardscape, and the colors, contrast, and condition of the plants is foremost.*

2.5-GALLON IWAGUMI-STYLE TANK. *This aquarium style seeks to emulate nature through the use of simple shapes and clear focal points. The use of just three rocks, two types of plants and very few small fishes conveys the sense of quiet harmony and simplicity that is the essence of the Iwagumi school of Japanese gardening.*

Hardscape, such as rocks and sunken driftwood, usually plays a role in framing the aquascape or helps to create flow. Nature-style aquascapes are often also one of three shapes: concave shaped, convex shaped, or triangular. Concave means that the height of the plants slopes down to some central low point, then climbs back up. Convex is the opposite of concave, and is often called an "island" shape, because the plants are low on either side

33-GALLON TANK. The Nature aquarium style, immortalized by aquatic visionary Takashi Amano, interprets natural landscapes with aquatic plants, hardscape, and carefully selected animals. Rather than a mixed community of fishes, an impressive school of one species is often stocked, such as the lovely grouping of Cardinal Tetras in this tank. Other livestock favored by Amano include freshwater shrimps such as the Amano Shrimp (Caridina japonica).

40-GALLON TANK. A Nature-style aquascape can perfectly mimic any number of scenes from nature. Whether it's a mountain range, pasture, forest, or even a babbling brook, the inspired Nature-style designer will duplicate the scene perfectly with mosses and ferns, plants and animals, colors and shapes, and always, a peaceful harmony among all the elements.

but high in the middle. Finally, triangular-shaped aquascapes are shaped like a right triangle, and the height of the plants slopes gradually from high on one side of the tank to low on the other. In most Nature-style aquascapes, there is only one main focal point and it is almost always positioned according to the Golden R~~~ Natural appearance, flow, and other Japanese gardening ~ are most important.

The theme of the **15-GALLON IWAGUMI-STYLE AQUARIUM** is simple tranquility. "Iwagumi" means rock formation in Japanese garden style. The number of rocks, and how and where they are placed are fundamental to the theme. Also important are the limits on the number of plant and animal species, one or two only, which maintain the quiet peace of the scene.

29-GALLON AQUARIUM

Background: Rotala macrandra 'Green', Ludwigia arcuata, Pogostemon yatabeanus, Limnophila aromatica, Cyperus helferi.

Midground: Ludwigia senegalensis. Rotala *sp. 'Mini'*, Anubias nana, Pogostemon helferi, Lobelia cardinalis 'Small Form', Eriocaulon cinereum.

Foreground: Hemianthus callitrichoides.

Equipment: *100 watts of light via 65-watt Power Compact and additional T5s for 9 hours. One canister filter. Pressurized CO$_2$ via ceramic diffuser. Substrate: Eco-Complete.*

Fertilization: *Dosing via autodoser, dry fertilizer with NPK; Flourish, 1 ml per day.*

Fauna: *Harlequin Rasboras (Rasbora heteromorpha), Neon Tetras (Paracheirodon innesi), Cardinal Tetras (Paracheirodon axelrodi), Cherry Shrimp (Neocaridina sp.), Nerites Snails (Neritina sp.).*

This **2.5-GALLON** *uses Blyxa japonica and* Anubias nana *in the* **background**; Echinodorus tenellus var. 'Tenellus', **midground**; *and* Eleocharis acicularis *and* Riccia fluitans *in the* **foreground**. **Lighting:** *18-watt Power Compact for 8 hrs; do-it-yourself CO$_2$.* **Filtration:** *hang-on-back;* **Substrate:** *Aquasoil.* **Dosing:** *NPK when needed.* **Fauna:** *Cherry shrimp (Neocaridina sp.).*

55-GALLON AQUARIUM

Background: Rotala *sp. 'Colorata'*, Alternanthera reineckii *'Rosaefolia'*, Blyxa aubertii, Ludwigia inclinata *var.* verticillata *'Cuba'*, Pogostemon stellatus.

Midground: *Eriocaulaceae 'Type 2'*, Blyxa japonica, Anubias nana *'Golden'*, Anubias nana, Rotala verticillatus, Cryptocoryne pontederiifolia, Cryptocoryne wendtii *'Red'*, Hemigraphis traian.

Foreground: Cryptocoryne parva, Pogostemon helferi, Ranalisma rostrata, Echinodorus tenellus *v. 'Tenellus'*. Fissidens fontanus, *affixed to the dense, sinking Manzanita driftwood.*

Equipment: *110-watt Power Compact light for 9 hours; Aquasoil substrate; pressurized CO_2 with glass diffuser; 2 canister filters; small powerhead for extra water circulation.*

Fertilization: *NPK three times a week, 5 ml Flourish three times a week.*

Fauna: *Cherry Shrimp (Neocardinia sp.), 15 Rummy-Nose Tetras (Hemigrammus rhodostomus), 12 Ember Tetras (Hyphessobrycon amandae), 10 Green-Flame Tetras (Aphyocharax rathbuni), 2 pairs Apistogramma borelli, 3 Bristle-Nose Plecos (Ancistrus dolichopterus), Nerite Snails (Neritina sp.).*

SCIENTIFIC NAME INDEX

SCIENTIFIC NAME INDEX

SELECTED BIBLIOGRAPHY

Amano, T. 1994. *Nature Aquarium World*, Book 2.
T.F.H. Publications.

Amano, T. 1994. *Nature Aquarium World*, Book 3.
T.F.H. Publications.

Barber, T., Wilson, R. 2005. *The Simple Guide to Planted Aquariums*.
T.F.H. Publications.

Brunner, G. 1963. *Aquarium Plants*. T.F.H. Publications.

Hiscock, P. 2003. *Encyclopedia of Aquarium Plants*.
Barron's Educational Series, Inc.

Huckstedt, G. 1963. *Water Chemistry for Advanced Aquarists*.
T.F.H. Publications.

Kasselmann, Christel. 2003. *Aquarium Plants*.
Krieger Publishing Company.

Rataj, K., Horeman, T. 1977. *Aquarium Plants: Their Identification,
Cultivation, and Ecology*. T.F.H. Publications.

Scheurmann, I. 1987. *Water Plants in the Aquarium:
A Complete Owner's Manual*. Barron's Educational Series, Inc.

Stodola, Dr. J. 1967. *Encyclopedia of Water Plants*.
T.F.H. Publications.

Sweeney, M. E. 1990. *Aquariums for Your New Pet*.
T.F.H. Publications.

Sweeney, M. E. 1999. *The Guide to Aquarium Plants*.
T.F.H. Publications.

Walstad, D. L. 1999. *Ecology of the Planted Aquarium*.
Echinodorus Publishing.

Weigel, W. 1964. *Aquarium Decorating and Planning*.
T.F.H. Publications.

Yoshino, S., Kobayashi, D. 1996. *The Natural Aquarium:
How to Imitate Nature in Your Home*. T.F.H. Publications.

RESOURCES

Aquatic Gardening Association:
www.aquatic-gardeners.org/info.html

UK Aquatic Plant Society: *www.ukaps.org/*

COMMON NAME INDEX

CREDITS

DESIGN Linda Provost

COLOR Digital Engine

EDITING James M. Lawrence, Emily Stetson

**Contribute your comments and suggestions
for future editions of this book:**

www.microcosm-books.com

PHOTOGRAPHY CREDITS

MATT WITTENRICH 7, 23, 24, 25, 36, 37, 42, 44, 46, 47, 55, 60, 76, 97, 103, 121, 173

MP & C PIEDNOIR 10, 27, 59, 63, 65, 66, 74, 75, 77, 78, 85, 87, 88, 92, 94, 98, 99, 101, 102, 104, 106, 113, 119, 144, 171, 175

JEFF UCCIARDO 12, 18, 21, 22, 28, 40, 48, 50-51, 54, 57, 71, 105, 108-109, 111, 112, 114, 122, 124, 126, 138, 141, 145, 147, 148, 149, 153, 180, 181, 182-183

BEN TAN, AQUASPOT WORLD 13, 58, 60, 61, 64, 71, 72, 73, 79, 81, 84, 85, 86, 87, 88, 89, 90, 91, 93, 96, 99, 101, 102, 103, 104, 115, 116, 120, 122, 127, 132, 133, 134, 136, 138, 146, 147, 150, 153

NEIL HEPWORTH 14, 26, 30, 31, 32, 33, 116, 118, 123, 128, 130, 151, 172

GEORGE FARMER 16, 17, 33, 34, 38, 41, 43, 52, 107, 131, 155, 166, 169, 176, 177, 178, 179, 180

JAN BASTMEIJER 82 (Wiki Commons)

DIANA WALSTAD 49

FLORIDA AQUATIC NURSERY 62, 67, 69, 70, 80, 90, 98, 100, 126, 129, 135, 137, 139, 140, 142, 146, 152, 156, 160, 161, 162, 163

AARON NORMAN 68, 110, 117, 136, 154

K. TANAKA 45 (Wiki Commons)

ROBERT PAUL HUDSON, AQUABOTANIC 125

TIM PFEFFER 143

NEALE MONKS 168

Mary Sweeney is a lifelong naturalist who grew up—and still lives—in the Two Rivers area of the Jersey Shore. She has been watching, collecting, and keeping fishes since early childhood.

She enjoyed a 15-year career in medicine, but changed course midstream and was employed in the Editorial Department at T.F.H. Publications for nearly 20 years. She is the former editor of *TFH* magazine, and has written countless books, articles, and columns on aquatic life. She has enjoyed giving talks on discus and other aquarium topics at aquarium society events all over the U.S. Her writing has appeared in *Tropical Fishkeeping*, *Aquarium Fish International*, and *Pet Age*, among others. She is currently a managing editor of *Microcosm Aquarium Explorer* (www.microcosm aquariumexplorer.com), a Web resource for freshwater and marine aquarists.

Now Mary works from her home, the historic Water Witch Club, in Monmouth Hills, New Jersey, where she lives with her husband John, son Eamonn, faithful canine companion Daisy, and an assortment of piscine pets. She enjoys life between the ocean and the woods, surrounded by garden and wildlife.